PRAISE FOR DAVID LYONS

David Lyons, an experienced former homicide detective, has provided a primer on cold case/ homicide investigations that is geared towards the true crime audience. True crime fans have increased exponentially over the years due primarily to the popularity of Podcasts. This book is a must read for fans of the true crime genre, who want to better understand the mechanics behind the investigation, as well as why the police are sometimes reluctant to discuss active cases with civilians.

JOHN SCHWARTZ, NYPD DETECTIVE 1ST GRADE (RETIRED)

True Crime and Consequences ignites a long-overdue conversation about the razor-thin line between curiosity, tenacity and obsession in the pursuit of justice. Blending sharp wit, unflinching truths and hard-hitting facts, it dives into the complex world of solving open murder cases at a time when true crime has become both a cultural fixation and a stark reality for those still seeking answers. For many, the genre is entertainment—a way to pass the time, unwind or spark conversation. But for victims and their families, these stories aren't just headlines or case files; they're lived nightmares that demand respect, care and relentless dedication.

KRISTEN PFLUM FORMER TV NEWS REPORTER AND HOST OF THE EDWARD R. MURROW AWARD-WINNING PODCAST TAKING ALEX

David's book provides insightful information about how members of social media groups such as the one I created can really make a difference in providing assistance to families and law enforcement alike! We all have the same mission:" Bring our missing home and justice for our murdered.

SANDRA HASTY, MOTHER OF MISSING
ADULT PRESUMED DEAD.

True Crime and Consequences serves as a bridge between the True Crimers and the Police Department. David lays out a clear path to open communication so that both parties can realize their common goal, work together, and make sure justice is appropriately administered. As a Murder Cop, himself, David is the perfect person to write this long overdue book. True Crime and Consequences will help close a lot of open cases.

SCOTT HARVEY SPEAKER, COACH,
AUTHOR OF SILENCE KILLS

When my brother went missing 10 years ago, my family and I were in blind panic. Since then, we have been determined to leave no stone unturned. David's book is a must-read for families like mine. It provides an omniscient overview of how we can all effectively assist law enforcement without burning bridges and overstepping boundaries.

JENNIFER GORLEY COFFEY, SURVIVING
FAMILY MEMBER

TRUE CRIME
& CONSEQUENCES

TRUE CRIME
& CONSEQUENCES

DOES THE TRUE CRIME COMMUNITY
HELP WITH MURDER INVESTIGATIONS
OR HURT THEM?

DAVID LYONS

EMPOWERED
PRESS

CONTENTS

Published in the United States by Empowered Press Publishing, Melbourne, Florida.

ISBN: 978-1-957430-31-7 (paperback)

ISBN: 978-1-957430-32-4 (ePub)

Library of Congress Control Number: 2025937461

http://theempoweredpress.com

Cover Design: Onur Aksoy

http://onegraphica.com

Layout Design: Jill Carlyle

The Empowered Press and our imprints can bring authors to your live event. For more information or to book an event, please email: publish@theempoweredpress.com

This book is dedicated to the victims of violent crime and the loved ones and survivors left behind. May we never forget the victims' names and keep fighting for genuine criminal justice to be delivered in a prompt and accurate manner.

In Memory of
Ray "The D.A." Larson
August 17, 1943 - August 1, 2021
"Okay. Get ready, buckaroo, we're going to trial."

Fayette County Commonwealth Attorney

DUNNING-KRUGER EFFECT

When a person's lack of knowledge and skill in a certain area causes them to overestimate their own competence.

PREFACE

Have you ever watched the early episodes of a reality TV competition? Whether it's a talent show, adventure race, or singing competition, there's always one contestant that just makes you cringe. During their one-on-one interview they're certain they are the expert and guaranteed to win. Their grandma is by their side. And maybe their cat. No offense, cat people. But as soon as they take the stage for round one, we all know the producers picked this guy for the ratings, not to win.

The truth is, any one of us can think we're an authority on any number of topics: the armchair quarterback, TikTok foodie, or home Jeopardy champion. We've got just enough experience—and passion—to act like experts, yet we don't know what we don't know. Pulling out a fantasy football win is a world away from carrying the weight of a head coach on Super Bowl Sunday. Posting a few videos of fancy food won't earn you a Michelin star as a chef. And it's easy to shout out Jeopardy trivia from the comfort of your couch versus remembering to answer in the form of a question while in the TV spotlight.

Any time a person's lack of knowledge and skill in a certain area causes them to overestimate their own competence, you see the Dunning-Kruger effect in action. Sometimes this cognitive bias works in reverse: those who truly do have an expertise find it so easy that they think everyone should master it in a moment. I see both sides of the bias come out in the true crime community, and either way it can have disastrous consequences on cases and survivors.

According to Therapist.com, there are four stages of competence:

1. **Unconscious incompetence:** You're ignorant of what you don't know.
2. **Conscious incompetence:** You're aware of what you don't know, but you haven't taken steps to learn more.
3. **Conscious competence:** You're actively learning and acquiring knowledge about a subject.
4. **Unconscious competence:** You've mastered a subject so extensively that you may forget or take for granted how much you truly know.

If you are a true crimer, I want to help you get to #3: actively learning and acquiring knowledge about investigations—more specifically, murder investigations—and the processes and procedures surrounding them.

If you are a murder cop, I want you to be able to work backward from #4 to meet the true crimer at #3, so we can all appreciate the value each side can bring and maybe even work together.

INTRODUCTION

Does the true crime phenomenon, and the people who make up the true crime community, help or harm murder cases and the surviving family members of the victims?

That's what we're about to find out.

We live in a hyper information age. Endless facts and findings are just a fraction of a second from our fingertips, and we all can offer up information at the same lightning speed. The true crime genre blasted into incredible popularity because of this lightning bolt of communication.

Tons of people have taken advantage of this opportunity, diving deeper into this ocean of information. Some folks move from curiosity into action—conducting investigations to help find the truth in the evilest criminal event we know, murder. And that is a good thing. The ability to use time, imagination, creativity, and maybe some untapped skills to find truths and deliver justice is awesome. As a former homicide detective myself, I am all for people pitching in.

Here is the problem: If any of this is done wrong, even if well-intentioned, the goalpost of justice may get moved further down the field—or may be torn down forever.

This is happening as you read this, and something needs to change as fast as possible. No exaggeration here: cases are suffering, and the families and friends left behind are being sent into the darkness, thrown into a community of survivors they never asked to be a part of.

I coined this book title, *TRUE CRIME AND CONSEQUENCES: Does the True Crime Community Help with Murder Investigations or Hurt Them?,* after watching a remarkable documentary titled *Don't F**k with Cats: Hunting an Internet Killer*. The crime film was skillfully produced and directed by Mark Lewis. It highlights some of the most passionate and creative amateurs that I have seen.

I was floored at the ingenuity the web investigators brought to the table. I was also moved by their candid frustration and anger when it came to bringing the fruits of their hard labor (yes, they busted their asses) to law enforcement. I can still smell the hot asbestos from the brake pads as their investigation slammed to an abrupt halt and hurled them into the windshield of disappointment like a squashed bug when they took their findings to the cops.

What really spoke to me about these passionate gumshoes was witnessing them make mistakes and, most importantly, own those mistakes and learn from them. Wow. What an incredible amount of humility. That will come up in this book, and it is important.

If you were one of the folks featured in the documentary, hats off to you—you have my sincere respect.

On the other side of the coin, and there is always another side, is the 2024 documentary *They Called Him Mostly Harmless,* directed by Patricia E. Gillespie. It's a well-produced story about unidentified remains found in Florida. While it delivers us some well-intended amateur sleuths, it also parades a bunch of goofy people in front of us that is nearly painful to watch.

If you have not done so already, go watch these documentaries back-to-back and you will see where I am coming from.

Now, what if someone with experience, but admittedly not all the answers, offered up a little book—kind of like a guide—on how all this works from the murder cop side? Could it help people with good hearts make a difference?

And what if murder cops took a look at this book, as well, to learn how to tap into the energy in the true crime community?

This is why I took the time to write this book.

I want to protect cases and survivors so that they have a clean shot in criminal court.

I want to protect people's rights (even if we loathe some of the defendants because of what they have done).

I want to protect *you*, the reader, from dangerous consequences, including your very reputation.

And at the same time, I want to encourage murder cops to listen to those in the true crime community, as many have their hearts in the right place.

For the sake of the victims and the survivors, don't you think it's at least worth trying? Turn the page and let's find out.

PART ONE
HOW'D WE GET HERE?

CHAPTER 1
IS THERE A PROBLEM, OFFICER?

AH, the infamous question every cop LOVES to hear. "Is there a problem, officer?" Give it a try the next time you get pulled over. I bet you won't even get a ticket. NOT!

If you are a true crime fan, you might be asking, "What gives, David? I love true crime and can't get enough of it. So seriously, what's the problem?"

If you like to investigate cases—a little or a lot—you might be offended that I would even suggest you could hurt a case—after all, you just want to help.

And if you're a murder cop... well, you probably just gave an eye-rolled *pffft*, and closed this book. Stay with me. (At least finish this chapter.)

I love solving a good true crime mystery. After all, my wife, Wendy, and I are the creators and co-hosts of *The Murder Police Podcast*, a project we started in 2020. One of our most meaningful series was "The Murder of Angela Owens Wooldridge." Angela was Wendy's literal best friend of over thirty years, and she was murdered by her husband in February 2022. These were difficult episodes to record and edit, but it was worth it in order to memorialize a beautiful woman and raise awareness about domestic violence. The true crime community provided a platform to honor the victim and potentially protect others.

But don't get me wrong—the cop in me takes the laws and procedures that must be respected while you solve a crime very seriously.

You heard that right—I gave twenty-eight years to my career in law enforcement. As a retired homicide detective, you better believe there is no greater responsibility than to protect victims and survivors and bring about justice. And I've got very little tolerance for yahoos who watch a few seasons of *Law and Order* and think they're experts.

Do I believe the true crime world can be a force for good? Yes. Curiosity is generally harmless. Helping on a case is commendable. But I also know that sometimes, too many times, things go sideways.

IF IT MAY PLEASE THE COURT

I don't expect you to take my word for it. Let's start with five real-life examples, and you tell me if the true crimers helped or hurt.

EXHIBIT A:

A young woman goes missing while traveling across the United States with her fiancé. She'd been sharing her adventures on social media when she suddenly went quiet.

An all-out, highly publicized investigation launched into full swing —including the shit show that took center stage on the 24-7 news cycle. The young woman was eventually found dead, and the case took on an almost surreal life of its own. Nearly rabid public interest filled the internet and television with ridiculous conjecture, opinion, theory, and flat-out hate. The fiancé was, of course, suspected and indicted in the court of public opinion.

Based on my experience, even from far away, this three-ring circus of unpolished clowns and asshats likely hampered some aspects of the official investigations that followed. And likely compounded the pain the victim's family was dealing with.

A mob mentality eventually erupted with angry protesters storming the front lawn of the house where her fiancé's parents lived, totally convinced they were complicit in the girl's disappearance and murder. For many in the true crime community, any thought of a presumption of "innocent before proven guilty" was long gone. The only people maintaining that concept were the police. Imagine that.

EXHIBIT B:

A major true crime podcast takes on the case of a woman struck and killed in a hit-and-run. She'd been walking alone on a rural road in the dark early morning hours when she was struck by a vehicle and died.

The car left the scene but was quickly identified and located. The driver, who was interviewed within hours, told police that she knew she hit something but thought it might have been an animal. Was the driver being completely honest? Maybe, maybe not. But based on everything the police had (as in, the law), the most she could face would be crimes associated with leaving the accident.

Eventually, toxicology reports for the woman who died indicated a high level of intoxication, a result that backed up witnesses' statements from earlier in the evening.

The podcasters interviewed the grief-stricken mother, who was, undoubtedly, struggling to wrap her head and heart around such an unfathomable tragedy—a loss with more questions than will ever be answered.

Almost as if scripted, this tragic hit-and-run took on new directions: The police agencies involved were incompetent, if not corrupt, and were covering up a murder.

The victim's ethnicity, even though it played no significance in the incident, was brought to the forefront so racism could be inferred. Because we know that makes everything more nefarious.

And the hit-and-run driver (innocent until proven guilty, anyone?) was named on the podcast and lambasted for racism based on social media posts (that included the names of her children), and other Sherlock Holmes caliber investigative techniques used by the podcast hosts.

At the end of the day, one woman is wrestling with the worst nightmare a mother could imagine: the sudden loss of her daughter. The other woman, who was driving the vehicle and struck the victim, is publicly indicted for murder, her innocent children dragged into the ring, throwing water into her grease fire of confusion.

EXHIBIT C:

A Facebook poster shares photos of a deceased person on a true-crime discussion page (conveniently as an anonymous poster). They were supposedly looking for opinions as to what caused the injuries seen in the photos.

The point? There isn't one.

This was a person with a grotesque curiosity who had no problem exploiting the violent death of another human being. Period.

Most people, including me, openly questioned the purpose of posting the photos. A few defended the action. As it turned out, the photos were related to a high-profile case that had not even gone to trial yet. *No one* should have had access to these gruesome pictures, much less shared them on the internet.

Could this hurt a case? Without a doubt.

Pretrial publicity can taint jury pools, which, in turn, reduces the likelihood of a fair trial or a solid conviction. Jury selection can become extremely difficult, which could find the defense attorney team seeking a change in venue (when a trial is moved to another town or city). Witness testimony can be put into doubt as well, given that these graphic pictures were floating around. Ultimately, the results of a trial may be compromised by reasonable appeals from the defense, the prosecution, or both.

Perhaps even worse, imagine if the photos were of someone *you* deeply cared about?

EXHIBIT D:

Two super sleuth true crime podcasters cover the unsolved murder case of a man in a small community, working their own "investigation" along the way.

What started out sounding like a decent awareness piece and a call to action for information quickly flamed out. The two people acting like they knew what they were doing were, in reality, completely clueless about death investigations. These Einsteins went toe-to-toe with the investigating agency: first, accusing the detectives of incompetence, and then huffing with disappointment that the detectives wouldn't set time aside to meet with them and "confirm their theories."

To make matters worse, the podcasters described some of the people close to the victim who could possibly be suspects. They didn't use their names, but in that small town, people knew who they were talking about.

Awesome. Send them underground. Remind them not to discuss the case with anyone. Whose side are these guys on?

Can I add that as a murder cop, I would already be looking at these suspects closely. If I were on this case, I'd be livid. And the family? I bet you five bucks they'll now be waiting longer for the justice they need so badly—if it ever comes at all.

EXHIBIT E:

In 2021, Websleuths member Gabi Mendler, from a town in central British Columbia, Canada, took an interest in a case regarding a man missing in Calgary, Alberta. Webslueths is an amazing internet forum with members who have incredible curiosity about all things murdered and missing; you should check them out.

Members offered some theories on a thread in the forum based on what was known at the time, and Gabi started down some rabbit holes as well. Gabi recognized similarities between the man's missing person profile and details of a John Doe, a victim of suicide, whose remains were found in Vancouver, Canada. Though the two were in cities hundreds of miles apart, the remains were discovered in the days immediately following the man being reported missing. She found

CCTV footage showing the similarities and had an inkling that, despite the travel time between Calgary and Vancouver, this could be a match.

Gabi contacted the Calgary Police with her information. And waited. Patiently.

She didn't have to wait too long. In just a handful of weeks, Gabi received a call from the Calgary Police Department confirming it was a match! How did the police determine they had linked the two instances together? You guessed it: DNA analysis. That said, Gabi certainly got the ball rolling.

WHAT ARE THE ODDS?

So, there you have it: in just one out of five examples, the true crime community contributed positively. Oh, sure, plenty of others thought they were riding in on the horse of justice, but did they protect the victims? Or did they risk actually finding and convicting the killer? Did they care for the survivors? Or for the truth? Or did they care more for their fame, regardless of whether they were spewing misinformation?

In Exhibit E, three things stand out about the true crime fighters:

- Gabi and the other Websleuths had at least some kind of understanding that they were entering into a world larger than themselves.
- Gabi wanted to play by the rules.
- Gabi was motivated by the best of reasons with solid, good intentions.

I could list a dozen more cases, but I hope you get the picture. Because, as a former murder cop, there's nothing that makes my blood boil more than the re-victimization of survivors and the screwing up of investigations. Murder cops care deeply for the families they represent. We don't put our asses on the line to make it rich.

As Popeye once said, "That's all I can stands, 'cause I can't stands no more!" I am there. I have been getting there steadily over the years, but I can say I have arrived.

WHAT'S THIS MEAN FOR YOU?

Now I know you're sitting there thinking to yourself, "Yeah, but that's not me. I'm here for justice and truth. I care about the victims. I'm going to get them justice!"

I get it. I really do. But I'm not ranting because of where a person's curiosity and passion might lie. It's because I know all too well the damage even someone with a heart of gold can do to a case.

You know the old saying, "The road to hell is paved with good intentions." It's a real thing… even with our best intentions, things can go south in a hurry.

- Cases can be slowed down or destroyed. Too much or wrong information out and about can cripple a case or limit the chances it ever makes it to court. Cops don't hold information out of greed; they hold it because it protects people's rights while they are heading into criminal court. Jeopardizing a case isn't fair to the surviving victims' families and friends.
- Possible suspects can be run deeper underground. That's real. Blasting names or (dangerously) loose descriptions of suspects does nothing more than remind them to keep their heads low and avoid talking to the police. If a suspect hadn't thought of lawyering up yet, putting them on blast might give them a hint to do just that.
- If you shoot from the hip with opinions, you could create false narratives and misinformation, looking like an idiot or a moron in the end.
- Criticizing the efforts of the police investigations can cause real pain to a surviving family that is already hurt and confused. What they need is truth, even difficult truth. Propping up delusions or misinterpretations is simply cruel. If you are not

qualified to evaluate efforts and investigations, it's best to zip it. We'll discuss this further when we examine the motivations of individuals who wish to become involved in cases.

- Evidence can become unusable or harder to get accepted in court, and you could wind up in trouble for obtaining it or handling it.
- You could get your butt sued. Everyone has an opinion and a right to talk about the opinion. Opinions are hardly anything like facts, though, and can have nothing to do with the truth. No matter how much you believe in "your truth," there is only one in the eye of the criminal justice system. Spouting your truth might make *you* feel better, maybe even virtuous (news flash, you're not), but if you cross the line, you could end up in court yourself.

HANG ON TIGHT

We are going to hit some prickly topics here. I am going to talk about biases we all have and why we need to check them at the door. I will discuss the differences between concepts such as leads and theories, and conjecture and guessing versus opinions, exploring where these concepts are applicable and where they are not. And you need to know because investigation time is limited and priceless, and nobody, I mean *nobody*, is in the mood to waste a second of it.

You are going to need a thick skin: we will talk about the pitfalls of emotions and feelings in this work, and why they don't belong.

I am going to start with a hot topic right off the bat: justice. What is it? Are there different types? Does the hunt for one kill the other? Spoiler alert: it very well could.

I will be talking about the things law enforcement gets wrong (likely piss a few coppers off) and why, so we all have skin in the game.

And again, for my cop friends, I want you to open your minds as well. You and I both know that most of the cases we see get solved are laid down because of information we received from people in the community. Why not dig a deeper well that we can all drink from?

WHAT'S THE GOAL?

This is not a course on how to be an investigator. It's just a conversation between you and me about what the real world looks like. But should it spark an interest in your becoming an investigator, you'll get an idea of what lies down that road, too.

If you are a member of the true crime community, I'm going to take you into the police world. I want to educate you about the basics of criminal investigations, especially death investigations. I'm also going to provide you with some tools to sharpen your critical thinking skills, so that you can approach what you see and hear from a genuine investigative perspective.

If you are a creator in the true crime genre, I might be able to keep you from looking like a fool. You'll help crime victims, rather than hurting them in the end. Another goal is to help you improve communication with murder cops in a case (and vice versa) and develop trusting relationships. I have seen enough so far to know that without an understanding of where we are all coming from, these relationships have a snowball's chance in hell. You do want to land that interview, don't you?

As I talk about barriers to getting to know a murder cop, just keep in mind I am not giving you argument points or excusing bad or frustrating behavior; I am helping you understand how the guts of this clock we call a police department are put together.

If you are a cop or a murder cop, this is for you, too. The law enforcement industry needs to learn to work with new sources of information.

So, hang in there with me. Open your mind and turn the pages with a willingness to see from a different point of view. Crazy thought: maybe we can start making room for us all to work together to find the truth and advocate for victims? How about that?

I know, and the next thing you'll know, we'll catch that Ted Bundy guy.

CHAPTER 2
LOST IN TRANSLATION

IF THE TRUE crime community has a place in finding truths, seeking criminal justice, and helping survivors—which I honestly believe they do—then we need to make sure we're speaking the same language. The conversation isn't going to go anywhere if we don't work from the same definitions. Consider this chapter your pocket guide to key roles and terms.

Let's get the biggest term out of the way first: justice. There are a thousand definitions of this hot-button word. I want to lay out what criminal justice is compared to other terms that borrow "justice"—because criminal justice is where the focus should be in crime investigations.

Before steam starts coming out of people's ears, let me jump ahead and say that when the criminal justice system is allowed to practice as it has always been *supposed* to, it inherently supports most of its other justice cousins. That said, some of the pushes for the other justice cousins actually screw up the justice system. Sorry. Just when I had some people calming down a bit, I said that.

THIS THING CALLED *JUSTICE*

Restorative justice, procedural justice, social justice, vigilante justice, street justice, retributive justice, distributive justice, political justice, economic justice, legal justice… the list goes on. Unfortunately, many of these have varying definitions, depending on who you ask. One doesn't though, and that's *legal justice* (the criminal justice system of the United States).

I'll argue till the cows come home that legal justice can accomplish several of these on the list, the ones that are inherent to what it means. For example, the criminal justice system is literally based on procedural justice, the best in the world. The confusion comes when people look at the process from an emotional viewpoint. For some folks, if the result of the justice system didn't soothe a conscious, then it must be flawed.

Social justice can be found in the system when judges are elected by community members and grand juries and trial juries are selected from the very communities where the offense occurred. Again, inject emotion and agenda and this just doesn't seem to be enough.

How about economic justice? The justice system should protect fair and balanced opportunities; it should look out for the little guy. Unfortunately, when pursued for its own sake, it can end up tearing down the justice system. For example, good-hearted efforts to severely reduce or eliminate bail amounts because "it's not fair" often end up making communities less safe. Similarly, passionate pleas to go soft on crime in order to even the economic score end up backfiring. Unchecked crime (i.e. a lack of consequences for offenders) breeds more crime and destroys local economies. Businesses leave for a fear of safety—or never locate in an area to begin with. Think about how many big stores like Target and Walmart have exited local markets, taking resources and jobs with them, because of safety concerns. And let's be candid, they don't build stores just so people can walk in and take what they want without paying. When it's operating right, legal justice should support economic justice.

Even restorative justice is intended to be found in the system: plea bargains, probation, parole, and opportunities to divert into treatment programs. In the end, criminal defendants aren't *owed* anything; they are, by the Constitution, entitled to a long list of rights and protections. All of these are legit, but ironically enough, crime victims have hardly anything in the works to "restore" their lives.

When the system isn't enough, people want to change it. I get that. But are those efforts helping? Or making matters worse? That's what we're here to figure out.

I just hit these types of justice from 36,000 feet and did so at a distance on purpose. I am not here to bicker about the specific wording of a definition, but I do hope you can see the limitations of each of these individual justices. They only entertain a single argument, a single angle and intent, and life doesn't work that way. Our criminal justice system is the real deal.

Defining Legal Justice

It boils down to two types of justice: *criminal justice* and what I call *virtue justice*. And criminal justice is the only one that matters.

Virtue justice is the quick and vengeful justice some people want. Its gavel falls to raw emotions instead of facts and processes. For the person that seeks virtue justice, the rewards are off the hook. Elevating "their truth" above all others—the perception of being right that is amplified by others being wrong—they get their fifteen minutes of fame, fortune, and pride as they hear their own voice screaming from the mountain tops.

While virtue justice may feel good, it has little or nothing to do with criminal justice and, in reality, is more like a wrecking ball. Seekers of virtue justice cannot be objective. They suffer from confirmation bias, making the same horrible mistakes that untrained and unseasoned cops might make. They swing their sword wildly and leave a trail of pain and damage along their path.

In the end, you have to choose which kind of justice you want to see. If blurting your feelings, damning people based on your emotions, or being right even if you're wrong works for you, then go on with virtue justice. But understand, you will likely hurt the criminal justice that we've all agreed is the system. If you're the victim, satisfaction should (but won't) be easy. And if you are speaking for other people, shame on you. That's selfish and narcissistic.

At the end of the day, social advocates want the criminal justice system to work. We all want the criminal justice system to work.

Let's play this out.

Say you catch wind of an unsolved murder. You see posts and news articles online, charging up your emotions. "Where's the justice?" So, you roll up your sleeves and get to work. You sleuth around and crack the case! (At least you *think* you cracked it.) Whoo-hoo! The *truth* is out now (thanks to YOU). *You're* famous!

The question is, how did all this *truth* come out? Was it on your vlog, or in a criminal courtroom? Was it airtight, legally obtained, and able to successfully secure a conviction of the RIGHT people who were truly responsible for the crime? It only takes one wrong step for that perfect evidence to be inadmissible or the illegally obtained confession to cause a mistrial. You can point and shout all day long, but without process and procedure in a court of law, the bad guy is gonna get away with it.

Listen. I am a retired cop who spent years seeking truth and justice for victims. Hell, I commanded an entire section of investigators of all types that included murder cops before I retired. When my wife and I are producing content for *The Murder Police Podcast*, we cover some unsolved cases that get my murder cop wheels turning. I can come up with a list of investigative routes and tasks faster than you can tweet (or X, or whatever it's called these days). You better believe I'd roll up my sleeves and pound the pavement to see the bad guy behind bars— but I stop. I'm retired. I'm out of the game. Sure, the ideas and strategies I have are solid; the outside perspective could very well make a difference. But the harm I could do to the cases greatly outweighs the potential good.

I have to remember: Don't hurt cases!

If you are a member of the true crime community and your intentions are truly good, then please come on board. Learn the rules, build relationships, and be part of a healing process that makes sure justice is served. There is a place for you to help if you'll allow me to show you how.

I am going to focus on criminal justice from here on out, but you will see the signs of virtue justice as we move along. I won't point them out all the time; your blossoming investigative skills will spot them as clear as day.

What Justice is NOT

Now that you understand what justice is let's set the record straight on what justice is not. This is just as important because if the air is not clear, problems start, and frustrations grow.

Justice is not a commodity. It can't be bought or sold. It can't be demanded, petitioned, protested, or rioted into existence.

Justice is not a quick fix. It's not a hamburger that you can customize to "have it your way," and it's certainly not like the pizza you can get delivered "in 30 minutes or less." The wheels of justice turn slowly on purpose. The goal is getting to the truth, and the truth can be like finding a needle in a haystack. It demands as much accuracy as possible to protect the rights of *everyone* involved.

Justice is not a place to conduct social experiments. Sadly, unrealistic policymakers use it to play games. At the least, people feel frustrated, and at worst, they get hurt.

Justice is not a place for emotions—it is a place for facts that come from impartial investigation. It's not a place for unleashing bias or revenge. It's not a place for the unethical or shortsighted. Justice isn't found in a crowded room filled with guesswork and conjecture. It's not a game or there for anyone's entertainment. Justice is, in the end, simply what's just.

CHAPTER 3

WHO'S WHO

NOW THAT WE all understand the goal is criminal justice, let's talk about who's who in this true crime world.

I'm going to use the word *survivor* a bunch in this book. This is a critical role to define.

I think it's also important to define *the true crime community* and the roles it plays—good or bad. We're also going to talk about the *true crimer*, the individuals involved in this community. There are several roles an individual can play, and they each come with their own risk and reward.

"What about the victim," you ask? "Aren't you going to advocate for victim's rights?"

For the most part, we are going to be talking about murder in this book. After all, it is the biggest interest in the true crime community. And I hate to say it, but in a murder case the victim is gone. They've been taken by evil hands and evil deeds. Who's left behind needing justice? The survivors.

SURVIVORS

Every heinous act of violence triggers a tsunami of pain for someone. Most obvious are the loved ones, close family, and friends left behind to pick up the sharp, broken pieces of a puzzle that hurt too much to handle and rarely complete the picture.

Others include the people who didn't die but were close enough to be left emotionally wounded by these horrible acts of evil. These are the people who may have witnessed the victim's death, perhaps narrowly avoiding being killed themselves. Think of everyone impacted at a mass shooting: This could be students, teachers, aides, and admin, or even the bus drivers and cafeteria crew on site. This includes the customers and co-workers in the wrong place at the wrong time in the robbery or drug deal "gone bad." I hate that term. When would we argue that a robbery or drug deal could "go good?"

Survivors are a group of people forced to join a club they never wanted to be in. They are special people and deserve more than they usually get. For a murder cop, they are the most important people from the moment the cop picks up a case.

Survivors drive the murder cop to bring answers. Every minute of working the case aims to resolve the madness they were thrown into by securing an arrest and conviction. They'll work both on and off duty because the case is always on the murder cop's mind until justice is served.

Don't call it closure. People throw that word around when they talk about justice and survivors, especially when arrests are made. It's well-intended—but it's wrong.

According to Dr. Greg Davis, a forensic pathologist and friend and mentor of mine, survivors never get closure. At best, they start to metabolize the loss, but it will be part of the fabric of who they are for the rest of their lives. Personally, I think Greg nailed it; it's what my survivors have experienced over the years.

Survivors get the absolute worst news that anyone can ever receive, and their lives start to revolve around fear, anger, frustration, pain, and incredible grief. They just got pushed into the meat grinder that the criminal justice system can be because, as good as the system is, it is brutal on a survivor. In the end, the appropriate word for what this experience comes down to is trauma—nothing short of raw trauma.

And in the murder cop business, these survivors have a right to be frustrated, angry, and impatient. Murder cops accept that and offer themselves up in spite of it to help the survivor out. Note: this relationship is for THEM. No proxies, no virtue signalers interested in the case. The survivors. This will become clearer as you read on.

No matter how you came into this conversation, my challenge to you is to truly respect survivors and walk carefully around them and their journey. *Never* add to their pain. Ever. If you're a cop, visibly walk the talk and inspire the true crime community to do the same.

THE TRUE CRIME COMMUNITY

Fascination with villains and solving whodunits isn't new. While it may be exploding in popularity and accessibility with the advent of social media and mediums such as blogging and podcasting, the general public has been intrigued by crime stories for generations.

Just look at infamous figures like Billy the Kid, Jesse James, John Wilkes Booth, Jack the Ripper, Al Capone, Bonnie and Clyde, Jeffery Dahmer, John Wayne Gacy, Ted Bundy, Tommy Lynn Sells, and Ángel Maturino Reséndiz (OK, I added the last 2 serial killers because I worked those cases personally).

When did this public obsession with solving crime stories begin? And how did we get to the true crime phenomenon we see today? Let's take a look back in history to help us define the true crime community.

IN THE BEGINNING

There's no exact date that *true crime* started. Whether it's plain curiosity, a yearning for equity, or wanting the answers to the never-ending "Why?" it's safe to say humans have been interested in other people's wrongdoings since the beginning of time. Let's start at ground zero for murder: Cain and Abel.

The earliest form of public communication was oral storytelling; ancient communities used conversations around the cooking fire, ballads, songs, and public performances such as plays to learn and share information. Cain's murder of his brother, Abel, was passed down as oral history and later recorded in the Old Testament of the Bible. Greek and Roman history is full of other crime cases told in a similar fashion. It may be slow, but the conversation and the infatuation are nonetheless there.

The first watershed moment in communication and true crime came from the fifteenth-century invention of the printing press. Suddenly, oral history could be preserved and distributed to the common person. Crime stories were locked in and memorialized through pamphlets, magazines, books, and novels. There are theories that printed interest in crime can be traced back as early as the sixteenth century.

In the nineteenth and early twentieth centuries, the stories of the day found their way onto modern stages, including vaudeville. Both fiction and non-fiction crime stories created heroes and villains, often infamous.

Newspaper headlines also capitalized on cases of murder and mayhem, responding to a growing audience of interested people. The media was cooking it up in the kitchen as fast as they could to meet the growing consumer appetite—a trend that has never stopped. A local reporter once told me, "If it bleeds, it reads." Few truer words have ever been spoken. Human tragedy draws an audience, which translates to dollar signs. Cha-ching.

The 1880s handed the world another gift: moving pictures. Guess what types of stories quickly became popular? Yep. Crime. In 1895, the Edison Company produced the short picture *The Execution of Mary Stuart*, showing the execution of Mary Queen of Scots. It is the first known use of special effects.

Things were on fire in the 1920s. Movies gained a voice when sound was introduced to give us "talkies," while commercially available radio broadcasts began to bring news to the masses in record speed. Families, and even neighbors, gathered together around "the wireless" to listen to music, news, and newly created entertainment programs. What is this dark magic?

Suffice it to say, communication was at a level earlier generations could never imagine. All the world was becoming a stage, and crime stories assumed the spotlight. Radio and movies were building a movement.

While everyone was rolling in all this new-fangled technology like a hot pig in cool mud, it got better. Again.

Television. By the 1930s, television technology became more polished and "talking pictures" could be fed directly to private homes like the old wireless. Holy cow! This technology flew at light speed. Black and white, then color. Cable, then satellite. Information was faster than ever, getting clearer than ever, and quickly affordable for the average Joe.

THE TRUE CRIME PHENOMENON EXPLODES

Fascination with crime stories hit a new level in the late 80s and 90s, when television networks and newly founded cable channels started producing a prolific number of true crime shows. Entertainment has never looked back.

America's Most Wanted (*AMW*) set the fire. John Walsh—a survivor himself, who lost his young son to a horrific abduction and murder—invited millions of people to join the search for the evilest people on the planet.

The show not only helped catch killers on the run, but it also took people deeper into the world of investigations. The audience got a taste of the synergy and momentum of investigations.

When my murder case was in production with *AMW*, my producer shared some tidbits that spoke volumes about the public's interest in crime. She told me the network made little money off the show. It had no value in reruns, unlike most TV shows, because the material dated itself when it aired. Yet whenever the network considered moving away from the show, millions of people angrily objected. The show stayed on the air because of the popularity, running for 23 years before the plug was pulled! And to be fair, similar shows took its place.

And then came THE INTERNET.

This is where we live today. In historical context, the technology is relatively new, yet it's hard to imagine life without it. If you were born after 1991, you've never known life without the World Wide Web.

News is instant, personal communication is instant, and the fascination with crime is now blogged, vlogged, posted, streamed, and shared with the tap of a finger. And here's the kicker: anyone who wants to can do it.

So today, there really is a thing called *true crime*. While there are a variety of definitions of true crime, there are three things that it always includes:

- Real, true-life acts of evil: typically violent in nature, and most often centered around murder or people that have gone missing under questionable circumstances.
- Criminal cases that are solved or unsolved (cold cases): either new or past cases, but unsolved cases drum up the most interest and examination.
- Cases that have made it to the public forum: written media, podcasts, vlogs, television, and streaming series or film. To say that cases "make it" to the media might be an understatement; many do nothing less than explode into the presence of the world.

Other crimes can be found in true crime—if the offense is sensational enough—but the taking of someone's life drives curiosity the most: the how, the why, and the innate yearning for justice. For most people, it comes down to wrapping their mind around how people can do awful things to one another. Others find the fear factor entertaining, much like going to a haunted house, with adrenaline dumps around every corner.

True crime has been categorized into a genre, but it looks bigger than that. It is more like a movement, with individuals and groups of people getting involved in solving cases and exposing wrongful convictions. Involvement includes anything from just talking about a particular case with friends, to rolling up your sleeves and getting involved. For many it's a real passion; a cause.

There is no doubt that a true crime culture has formed with many sub-cultures, mostly divided by people's level of interest and involvement. Just like any culture and value system, there are good and bad.

True crime is as hot as an oven. Almost every media provider gets this and is trying to get in on the action. It's a smart move: get it while it's hot!

BLOGGING AND VLOGGING AND PODCASTS, OH MY!

The biggest delivery vehicle for true crime content is blogging, vlogging, and the explosion of podcasts. Ironically, what began as oral traditions talked about in local communities, then moved into print and mass distribution, has returned to a spoken medium and brought a semblance of community back with it.

Information is available at the speed of light to a global audience, and access doesn't have a membership card. Even us everyday Joes and Janes can share information (and opinions) instantly.

The ether of the internet has spurred connectivity—comments and social media enable "conversations" to take place anywhere, anytime. "Community" forms around interest and opinion versus place. The online world made it possible for true crime communities to crowdsource a case faster than ever. All of this is amazing! But it comes with responsibility, as well—at least it *should*.

Blogging, vlogging, and podcasting have hardly any barriers to entry. Any one of us can jump in right now and never spend a dime to do so. (I'd go as far as to say that the true crime genre brought the biggest bump in the growth of the podcasting world.)

Podcasting is how I started to engage with the true crime community and share my experiences as a murder cop. On *The Murder Police Podcast*, we focus on education and victim advocacy (may they not be forgotten) by telling the story of a crime through the eyes of the people that investigate the case.

I certainly have learned a good deal of technical skills creating the podcast and a YouTube channel. But more importantly, I've learned more about who the true crime community really is.

WHO ARE "TRUE CRIMERS"?

To keep things simple, we need a cool name for the members of the true crime community. With all the respect in the world to those in the community, I am going to refer to these people as true crimers. It seems appropriate. So, regardless of your level of interest or involvement, you now have a name, at least in my book. Get it? My book? I'm here all night, please don't forget to tip the bartender.

All or Nothing

One of the first things I learned about true crime, and it led me into the community almost subconsciously, is the range of interest in this craze. People have either zero interest or they are all in. There's very little middle ground!

Case in point: When I'm out in public, I almost always wear something that advertises *The Murder Police Podcast*. Shirts, jackets, you name it. I am a big believer in guerilla marketing, to the point that I have left thousands of *The Murder Police Podcast* pens across the country. If someone sees what I am wearing and they are into true crime, they let me know.

True crime fans stop me in airports, hotels, and restaurants every time I travel. I've been stopped by flight attendants on planes and cornered by students or staff when I'm teaching leadership classes. Even if I'm not approached, I'll catch someone out of the corner of my eye, looking back and forth between their phone and our logo. No doubt, they are looking up the show. Bingo! That's at least one download, and downloads are the name of the game.

Does EVERYONE in the world LOVE *The Murder Police Podcast*? Of course not. True crime is a crowded genre and people have choices. Wendy and I are amazed we have a good-size audience in this competitive world. Time and again our listeners and fans tell us they are drawn to the authenticity and respect that we deliver: True crime. Real murder cops. Zero exploitation of the crime victim or survivors.

No matter what your role is in the true crime community, it should always be lived out with authenticity and respect.

What Does "Going Real Life" Mean?

Here it is, the big Kahuna.

One of the biggest hazards and harmful actions in the true crime community is "going real life." It looks like this concept was likely created in the true crime community, much like an organism that tries to heal itself. Enough people recognized some ridiculous behavior and gave it what I think is a very appropriate name.

"Going real life" is when a crimer leaves the discussion in a community and heads out to the real world with their opinions—and maybe much more. The crimer begins to contact survivors, suspects, witnesses, and, God forbid, even the families of the victims or the accused. Sometimes, the *real lifers* do so in the name of conducting their own "investigation," and sometimes simply to harass victims, suspects, and witnesses.

This "going real life" can hurt cases, and sometimes even be physically harmful to people. It's pretty clear that the responsible camps in the true crime community have seen this. Many true crime community social media pages and groups now prohibit "going real life" in their community guidelines.

Most true crimers say they're in it to help cases, not hurt them. If that's true, we need to talk about how to keep from going off the rails, even unintentionally.

The Voodoo, That You Do, so Well

So, what can a true crimer bring to the party? Not that we are looking for a straight up quid pro quo, but if we're all about justice and going to ride the mission together, we should take a look at what we each have to offer.

There is one gift that you true crimers have—and frankly, might make murder cops a little jealous of. It comes down to one word: time.

Time is super important. If I were still working cases, I would want you and your time on my side. Combine this little gem with imagination, critical thinking skills, objectivity, and virtuous intentions, and it's on like Donkey Kong.

There are not enough hours in the day for murder cops. I mentioned before that they work their cases whether they are on the clock or not, but 24 hours is always 24 hours. They're pulled in different directions, balancing multiple cases and responsibilities. As a true crimer, you have time. Take advantage of it. Use it wisely and efficiently. And above all, make it worth it.

Some of the most amazing results I have seen from the true crime community didn't come about because of vast resources of money or fancy equipment; it was the time they used to work through complex problems to find answers.

Let's not let this go to waste. There is a place for you.

CHAPTER 4
INTO THE DEEP END: WHAT KIND OF CRIMER ARE YOU?

ALRIGHT CRIME FAN, it's time to get personal. From curious bystander to outright activist, each true crimer has their own level of interest and involvement—and in turn, their own risks of hurting a case. You want to make a difference? Let's put reality to the test.

I am a big fan of John Maxwell. One of his philosophies that I love the best is understanding the difference between *success* and *significance*. Success simply means you've made it to the next level; significance means you've made a difference in someone's life.

There are limitless opportunities to be significant in the true crime community. Whether you're a person just dipping your toe to test the water or you've jumped right into the deep end, perhaps the bigger question is how to do so ethically.

Let's start by defining true crime roles and risks, then we'll take a look at how to check our intentions and keep our commitment to help and not hurt.

ROLES & RISKS

First off, this is not a license to start labeling others. You do you, boo.

These roles are not set in stone. In fact, you may identify with more than one, depending on the case or popular cause of the day.

They do give us a framework for evaluating what helps versus what hurts.

Notice the *Case Risk-O-Meter* rating for each role. This little gauge shows the potential for impacting a murder case and survivors (good or bad). Oh, and see if you can recognize a relationship between risk and "going real life."

Take a look and see for yourself:

The Interested: Like it sounds, the true crimer is interested in true crime, searching out material and killing time listening to or watching a show. It's interesting entertainment to this true crimer and not much more.

Case Risk-O-Meter reading: no potential risk to hurt a case or survivor.

The Curious: A little more than interest, now the true crimer takes in true crime with more depth, looking for answers to questions. This could be wrestling with good and evil, fairness in the criminal justice system, how the justice system works, or maybe, and hopefully in fewer cases, a morbid fascination with violent death.

Case Risk-O-Meter reading: little or no potential risk to hurt a case or survivor.

The Emotionally Moved: Building on curiosity, the true crimer has more of an emotional response to the cases they learn about.

Sympathy, empathy, sadness, fear (the haunted house adrenaline), frustration, anger, to name a few. These true crimers often put themselves "in their shoes" when it comes to the victim and survivors. While this can be a commendable take on a crime case, it can also be dangerous if emotions get highjacked (a loss of objectivity) or the true crimer's mental health becomes challenged, which is unfortunately a possibility. Take it from me, none of this is easy on anyone, including the murder cops that do the work. Please make sure you are looking out for both yourself and your true crime buddies with your mental and emotional health as you dabble in this dark world.

Case Risk-O-Meter reading: low to medium risk to hurt a case or survivor.

––––––

The Huddler: Now we see where the community begins. A true crimer that really is a fan won't be a fan alone, they will find other people to talk about cases with. Sometimes it's just a single friend, but it will often grow to something like a club, typically on the internet through message boards and social media platforms. As someone who worked in the death investigation business, I can see this as a truly enjoyable experience. I like following some of the conversations myself. Seeing people engaged in offering up opinions and theories in huddled sessions reminds me of what we would do in the homicide murder cop bay when we were working on a case.

Case Risk-O-Meter reading: medium risk to hurt a case or survivor. Risk starts going up because opinions might be getting published. If the intentions are good, and statements are factual, there's no problem. But if the intentions are not good, bad things could creep up, including insensitivity to a victim or survivors. Also, opinions and theories could make the rounds back to the tip line, forcing murder cops to follow up on clues that really weren't more than conjecture. You just robbed the murder cops of the limited and valuable time they need to follow real leads and work the case.

The Influencer: Some true crimers hit the internet or other media with their passion for true crime. They find a platform to speak from and share with bigger audiences. (This would describe *The Murder Police Podcast.*) Some of my favorite true crime podcasts live in this world. Responsibility comes into play at this point. Because of the platform, the legit influencers in true crime stay on the straight and narrow; they stick to sharing researched and defendable facts and are careful with conjecture and theorizing. And they never disrespect a victim. Irresponsible influencers, on the other hand, sensationalize unfounded rumors, gossip, and exploit the suffering of the survivors. They tend to develop, or at least spread, misinformation, simply for clicks and views. They might get their "fifteen minutes of fame," but cases and survivors pay the price.

Case Risk-O-Meter reading: moderate to high risk to hurt a case or survivor.

———

The Advocate Activist: When the true crimer becomes passionate about a case, they may get vocal. They have a global reach at their fingertips in today's world. The risk comes back to their intentions (good or bad) and their accuracy. Fighting the good fight for a victim, survivor, or criminal suspect is perfect. But the true crimer MUST be right. These folks can be downright scary. In the worst cases their emotions have been hijacked like a 1970s airliner and there is no objectivity, much less the ability to reason with them. They can be extremely reckless and often don't seem to care.

Case Risk-O-Meter reading: moderate to high risk to hurt a case or survivor.

The Amateur Murder Cop: Internet sleuth, armchair murder cop, private detective; this is the role of any true crimer that gets into the actual investigation of a case, to any degree. There is amazing value and potential here as long as it's tempered with a healthy dose of caution, understanding that this could also go sideways in a second if the amateur dick isn't careful and skilled.

Case Risk-O-Meter reading: high risk to hurt a case or survivor.

Do you find yourself in one or more of these roles? The deeper you go, the greater the risk. Helping versus hurting often comes down to motivation and intentions.

MOTIVATION & INTENTIONS

Let me warn you, my gentle reader—some of you may get prickly over this. That's alright. In fairness, there will be overlap when I talk about the intentions of murder cops, so be patient. I won't be throwing stones in a glass house.

Virtuous intention, the goal, isn't as lofty as it sounds. We don't need to cite ancient philosophers or academic texts; we are simply going to look at whether the true crimer, especially the amateur detective, is in this for the right reasons.

Trust me, when the true crimer approaches a murder cop with their findings, their intentions will be the FIRST thing the murder cop will be trying to figure out, whether they know it or not (they are police, so they are sneaky like that).

"Curiosity" is what most people will answer if you ask what motivates them, but that is not the same as intentions because it goes no further than inquisitive interest. And in turn, there is no action in the plans, so intentions really don't come into play. What I am talking about is what a person does with the results of where curiosity leads: do you simply want to learn and satisfy your questions, or do you want to get involved in a case? If so, you must answer the intentions question.

As you read the rest of the book, you will start to understand why you need to be honest with yourself. Virtuous intentions usually help people guard against bias and emotions. Less desirable intentions tend to invite bias and emotions and fuel them.

Take a look at this checklist. Which intentions are motivating your true crime involvement, regardless of your role:

A CHECKLIST FOR YOUR INTENTIONS

I want to be involved with a case because:

- I value the truth above all else.
- I want to help turn wrongs into rights.
- I am passionate about helping those that are helpless.
- I know what it's like to be a victim and can relate.
- My heart hurts for people lost in pain and darkness.
- I want to be part of something bigger than myself.
- I want to be part of a team that helps others.
- I want to be appreciated for my efforts.
- I want to be seen as a hero.
- I want to be famous and everyone to know me.
- If I can land a big clue, I will be a social media influencer.
- I think the criminal justice system is corrupt and want to prove it.
- I don't trust the police and want to be over their shoulders.
- I don't trust the police and would love to prove them wrong.I hate the police and everything they stand for.

Before you holler that this list is judgmental, think about it. Every one of these motives is alive and active in the real world. They're easier to spot than one might imagine, especially by murder cops working cases.

Do you see a problem brewing here? If you're anything beyond a Huddler but checked the last four intentions (or something like them), getting a murder cop to meaningfully engage with you will be next to impossible.

> "Ethical behavior is doing the right thing when no one else is watching
> —even when doing the wrong thing is legal."
> — Aldo Leopold

EXCUSES IN ACTION

American author and philosopher Aldo Leopold once said, "Ethical behavior is doing the right thing when no one else is watching—even when doing the wrong thing is legal." I'd venture to add it also means doing the right thing for the right reasons. If the reason for us to get involved is to seek justice for victims and survivors, it also means participating without any expectation of a return for your investment.

Your intentions are where your ethics, values, and character are defined. How they play out in real life is often more of a gray area than a clear-cut line. Let's be honest. You can easily convince yourself anything is "for the good"—that the end justifies your means. It's a slippery slope if you're passionate (translation: emotional).

If you really want to help more than hurt, watch out for these five common excuses, red flags that your ethics ain't so airtight.

Just Because You Can, Doesn't Mean You Should.

One of the best pieces of advice a senior police officer can offer new cops is simply, "Just because you can, doesn't mean you should." The goal for a new officer is to take training and experiences and translate that into wisdom. From that, cops learn how to use their discretionary authority ethically. Instead of seeing everything in black and white, there is a gray area that allows for dealing with each situation individually with grace and compassion. It's knowing how to focus on the big picture and maintain the goal of doing more good than harm.- Take a traffic stop, for example. One night on duty, a car sped past me. I flipped on my lights and siren. The driver cooperated and pulled off the road. I approached the driver as usual, and quickly learned that the woman at the wheel was not alone. She had a couple of kids in the car, and in the backseat was her distraught husband. He was in incredible pain and was literally dying from cancer, a long-fought battle from what his wife told me. Could I have written her a ticket for speeding? Absolutely. Did I? No, because I am not an asshole, and more than that, I cared about that family; I still think of them nearly three decades later.

Here is a more complex example. Let's say you're a murder cop investigating, you guessed it, a murder. You're knocking out some interviews with people that are close to the event, (witnesses, neighbors, co-workers, family, and such), and you get a guy in the box (interview room). After the general introductions and "why we're here" stuff, he quickly starts throwing himself closer to the center of the case. And then bingo! The next thing you know, he makes a direct confession to being involved in the killing. Sounds great, huh?

But you and your partner, who's also in the room, pick up on something. He seems a bit off mentally. You guys aren't psychs, but you weren't born last night either. By the letter of the law (all other requirements for the murder offense have been checked), you've technically reached the threshold of probable cause. That's enough to go ahead and arrest your new friend on the spot: take him straight from the interview box to jail, without passing go.

But you don't. Why? Because your ethical compass sees the problems—and getting it right is more important than getting a quick confession. So, you slow down, investigate some more, and then investigate more after that.

I saw this kind of scenario play out more than once in my career. My fellow murder cops and I didn't make an arrest, and we were proud of that ability to stop and think. I had one case where a young man admitted to being part of an arson crime that took the life of one firefighter and nearly killed a second. His mental health was a challenge for him, yet he was adamant that he was involved. We proved he was not. At the trial for the *real* suspect, the defense team tried to bring our false confessor's confession into trial. The judge denied it. I was told that a psychologist who had interviewed our friend came to the same conclusion. This guy was trying to be part of the wanna-be gang the true suspect was in, and in the end, needed help. Catching the right guy doesn't always equal the one with his hand up.

When we have botched cases and wrongful convictions at the hands of the police, this is usually where things went sideways. It's a fair criticism. Unfortunately, these incidents, though rare, are the ones that make the front page in the news.

By the way, doing the right thing by holding off on charging someone with murder when you have doubts is nowhere near as difficult as letting someone walk out of your interview room knowing they're the one, but you just don't have enough proof yet. Welcome to ethics.

Think Before You Act

What does this mean for you, true crimers? Think before you act. You may come across information (statements, photos, reports, etc.) legally obtained, but is sharing it publicly always the right thing to do? Whether you are the first person to come into the know or you simply see it on the internet, you have a choice. Do you keep it alive—even though you can hurt a survivor or hurt a case?

Case in point, the Delphi murder photos: Graphic crime scene photos from the 2017 Delphi murders in Carroll County, Indiana were leaked prior to trial. Victims of the double murder were 13-year-old Abigail Joyce "Abby" Williams and fourteen-year-old Liberty Rose Lynn "Libby" German. A suspect, Richard Allen, was charged with the murders in October 2022, and defense attorneys were appointed to represent him. (There is still no conviction at the time of writing this book.)

Fortunately, the leaked photos were delivered to Áine Cain and Kevin Greenlee who produce *The Murder Sheet* podcast. Ethical folks on that pod. They immediately turned the gruesome photos over to law enforcement. The two recognized the problems that these photos could cause for the case and did the right thing. You should give *The Murder Sheet* podcast a listen, it's well worth your time.

What if the photos had landed in less than ethical hands? After all, it's pretty darn likely that the goal of the leaker was to get them madly distributed across the internet.

If you received an envelope from an anonymous source with

photos like this, what would you do? If the pics popped up on your social media feed, would you even think twice?

"But Everyone Else Is Doing It!"

Have you ever heard a parent or teacher say, "If your friends jumped off a cliff, would you jump too?" Young or old, we're all influenced by others around us. Debating whether or not to join in or hold your own path turns even small decisions into ethical dilemmas. Sometimes we need the reminder to stay skeptical and hold true to our values and beliefs, even in the face of temptation.

One of the basic keys to solid ethics is having an ability to think about the long-term effects of our decisions and actions:

- Who am I and who might I become?
- What might happen to other people?
- Am I doing good or causing harm?

Back to the leaked crime scene photos scenario. If material like that gets leaked and goes viral, its very success is likely based on quick reactions without a lot of thought for the big picture:

- Groupthink (decisions made in a group that lack critical thinking and creativity)
- FOMO or 'fear of missing out' (feeling like you have to do something in order to keep up with others)
- Selfishness (taking every advantage to get attention for yourself)

How can you test your actions? The first thing is to ask whether the actions are defendable. Can we justify our actions and their repercussions—first to ourselves, then before family and friends, victims and survivors, and even potentially in court? "Everyone else is doing it" will never fly as a good defense.

Being the ethical person in the room might result in you being the only person in the room. When people give in to groupthink or operate in a pack mentality, they tend to distance themselves from people who don't agree. It can be difficult to stand alone, but it is one of the most commendable positions to take—especially when temptations and anxiety are knocking at the door. Don't be afraid to stand alone.

"It Isn't Wrong for Me to Want Them to Be Guilty."

This one turns my stomach every time.

A while back, I was watching a debate on a true crime social media page. It was a good debate—the kind of conversation that brings the true crime community together to discuss cases. One participant stood out in a sad way, though.

The case everyone was discussing had been laid to rest in court, and the conviction of one suspect meant the exoneration of another who had been drug through the social media mud for months. Despite the conviction of the real offender, this crimer wouldn't let go. I chimed in and made a polite remark that it wasn't fair to continue to beat on someone who was not involved. The response: "It isn't wrong for me to want them to be guilty."

It's horrible to want a particular person to be guilty of a crime, any crime, much less taking the life of another person. We want to find the RIGHT person.

It's fine to argue that the guilty should be punished (severely in my opinion), once the case is proven beyond a reasonable doubt, which is the standard in the US Justice System. Yet some people look at justice more like a horse race, an election, or a sporting event where we bet on winners and losers. And that takes us back to groupthink and a culture that inflicts harm and hurts people.

Ethically, what is missing here is anything remotely like objectivity and (specifically in the US) the presumption of innocence. Even murder cops maintain that objectivity and presumption during investigations until they cross over probable cause, charge someone, and prepare for trial.

You still think wanting a particular person to be guilty is harmless? Fine, if you keep your trap shut and your opinion to yourself.

Gotta Make Those Benjamins

It's sad that this one has to be said, but here we go. If everything you do is to become more successful at all costs, then it will cost you everything. There are few cases where the greedy desire to make more money or gain popularity ends well—once you sell your soul to the devil, the payments eventually come due.

People who focus on success often start to take shortcuts. They tell trivial lies or half-truths or even make stuff up on the fly to get the attention they think they need. Instead of handing information over to the authorities, they give it to the highest bidder. Can you imagine what some media outlets would have paid for the leaked Delphi murder case photos?

When this happens in the true crime community, critical case facts are spread on the internet, and people—who may or may not actually be involved—are indicted in the public view. The pain of survivors gets exploited, pouring salt into their wounds. The exhibits in Chapter 1 are perfect examples of this.

Can you ethically build an audience in the true crime community? You bet. Can you even make money? Absolutely! Just mind your P's and Q's, check your intentions and motivations, and be committed to help not hurt.

If we want to keep ourselves from slipping, we've got to start by being honest with ourselves. Trust me, it applies to murder cops, too.

CHAPTER 5
WHAT IS A MURDER COP?

SINCE WE TALKED about the true crime community, let's talk about the player I am going to call a murder cop.

A murder cop is someone who signed up for the J.O.B. It can be a cop, an investigator with a prosecutor's office, or an evidence technician—anyone on the law enforcement team.

Notice I stopped short of forensic scientist or analyst and medical examiner. That was intentional. One thing you will find is that the criminal court system is antagonistic—one side against the other—by wonderful design. One side makes a criminal accusation and carries the burden of proving it; the other side defends the accused person vigorously. In the middle sits the examination and analysis group, the roles that simply take evidence and data and deliver an objective opinion or finding without caring which side benefits.

If you want to play on the prosecution side of the fence—the side that catches the bad guys—you'll take an oath. This oath swears you to protecting the United States Constitution and *all* the people it protects. Then there's the rule book: the lines in the coloring book that you must stay in, the swim lane, everything that separates you from the civilian community and makes the civilian community your responsibility. And it is beautiful. The two together make the United States so much different than the rest of the world.

A good copper never sees this as a hurdle, or a barrier, or a pain in the ass. A real cop loves it and considers protecting it the reason they took the job. And they guard it. This is one reason they are slow to work with a civilian sleuth.

Truth be told, and I know some find this hard to believe, good coppers can't stand to work with bad coppers either. More on that is coming, I promise.

WHERE THE MURDER COPS LIVE IN POLICE DEPARTMENTS

I wanna talk to a cop! Don't we all? Kidding, just kidding.

If you've gotten into working on a case and come to the point where you want to speak to a murder cop (maybe you've got intel to share), it helps to have a rough idea about where they might be found in a police department or prosecutor's office. There are no hard-and-fast rules for this. It varies across the country, even city to city, but there are some basic foundations to how this might work.

For starters, the basic flow for a case should be simple:

1. A community member or cop sees a crime has been committed.
2. A report (offense report, crime report, incident report, etc.) is taken by a cop, highlighting the most serious offense (sometimes more than one law was broken).
3. That report routes through some kind of process in the department (this varies greatly) and finds an assignment "home" based on the offenses that were in the report.
4. Typically, the police department has a policy that tells everyone where certain offenses are assigned and investigated.
5. If a homicide has occurred, eventually a murder cop is assigned or "catches" the case.

How this report makes it through the department and to the detective (steps three and four) is a little more involved.

Size matters. The size of the organization, that is. Those of us that live in larger metropolitan areas (big cities), get used to having hundreds, if not thousands, of cops in our police departments. In actuality, big police departments are rare; the vast majority of law enforcement agencies in the United States are small, sometimes just a handful of officers and a chief or sheriff. In many cases, the chief is the single person in the police department.

According to a 2011 report from the Department of Justice (DOJ) studying data from 2008, they found that about half (49%) of all agencies employed fewer than ten full-time officers. The majority of departments are small; very few are as seen on TV. TV tends to highlight the bigger city police departments like Los Angeles and New York City, that have thousands of officers in their ranks. This can leave us with a false sense of reality, assuming our local police have almost endless resources.

You might think this data is a little old, but not much has changed and it's not likely to for some time. I see it every week when I'm teaching leadership development to brass across the United States. I'm working predominately with departments in this small to mid-size range.

Size impacts a police department in two ways: organizational structure and specialization. The smaller the police department, the more limited the structure is and the less likely it is to have the staffing for specialization.

For example, large departments can have sections in units with very in-depth specialties. They may have a homicide unit, a forensics unit, a photography unit, a victim's advocate unit, and more. These specialties help serve the community more effectively.

However, the smaller the police department, the more limited the structure is. These specialty options fade away. What we find most commonly around the country are departments where sworn and civilian members wear many hats, working several gigs. Do they get the job done? Sure. But resources are always stressed and those doing the job may not always get the specialty training that would be a big help.

This is where cooperation comes in. Small agencies may have detailed agreements (usually in writing) with larger neighboring departments. This allows them to borrow the services of the bigger agency in cases that overwhelm the smaller agency. This is very common, especially in violent offenses. It's also a growing trend is to ask other agencies to investigate officer involved shootings (OIS)—asking an outside agency to investigate provides an objective, independent review of the incident. It gives the community assurance there won't be conflicts of interest.

The city I policed in had a population well over 300,000 people, about 650 sworn officers, and a couple hundred civilian staff members. It was a common practice for our department to provide resources and assistance to the university police, as well as the smaller departments in communities surrounding our city. One of the most common things we would help with was providing forensic murder cops to investigate overwhelming crime scenes.

TAKE A NUMBER

Why should this matter to a true crimer? I'm glad you asked.

If you get yourself involved in an investigation and you ask to speak to a murder cop in Department A, there may not be one. Or whomever you get to talk to is a jack of all trades. Or you are forwarded to Department B.

You are not getting the run around—you're getting passed to the person assigned to the case. And they might not be in the building.

You can ask anyone your questions, but that doesn't mean they're at liberty to speak. Cooperative agreements typically lay out which agency can make public comments about a case, and to which parts they can even make a statement.

It might be annoying to you, but this chain of command is there to protect the case and the community. It is important to make sure information is as correct as possible and to prevent confusion. In most cases, the agency that takes the lead on an investigation will be the one to release information. So, if someone asks an assisting agency for info, they'll get told to talk to the lead agency.

If an officer in my agency was involved in an OIS, our state police agency was called in to conduct the investigation. While the investigation was underway, my police department would refer any questions to the state police. Again, it is not a run around. It is all about keeping the integrity of the case. So be patient.

Back to the big guys on the block.

In the bigger departments with a lot of specialization, the murder cop who caught the case could be nestled in a location that seems buried in the back office. If these looked like network paths, it'd route something like this:

Police department > Bureau of Investigation >General Investigations > Special Victims > Domestic Violence >Victim Advocate

Nobody is being *hidden.* It's not the old "needle in the haystack." In reality, this is a very efficient and effective plan to make sure the right team handles the case. Let's make it (more) complicated.

Some cases may be touched by several specialties. For example, in the murder of a child, it is common to have a Crimes Against Children murder cop come up front or co-investigate the case with a homicide murder cop. Though they are both assigned, they each have distinctive roles and tend to stay in their lanes.

Next, add in a forensic unit, photo and video unit, and maybe a task force, and you can start to see the breadth of this team.

Now you reach out to the police department and ask to speak to the murder cop assigned to the case so you can chat about your hard-earned information. Hmmm. What if nobody in the police department can find my murder cop?

In some cases, no one specific (a murder cop or officer) has been assigned to the case. Here is how this might look.

Sometimes a report was not taken and filed, at least yet. No report.

No murder cop has been assigned (yet). You are probably asking "WTF?!?!, it's a murder!"

Hang with me a second. This is a good opportunity to get inside the biz, because this is how it works in most police departments, across all types of crimes.

Some police department policies don't require a report for all criminal offenses or incidents. This is not uncommon for low-hanging fruit crimes or incidents that don't quite meet the requirements of a crime. Some police departments are satisfied with the record of the call coming to a dispatch center or things like arrest or offense citations. Examples might include a report of a gun being fired with no victim or damage (the call into dispatch is the record), or an arrest for a DUI (the charging document may be all that is needed).

Sometimes, somebody forgets to take a report. Yep. It happens, even with murders. Tons of cops show up on a shooting death in the street, and everybody assumes somebody else took the report. Maybe they even assume the homicide murder cops took the report! *Gasp*! Not on your ass! The bigger crimes usually get these worked out in a few hours or a day, but smaller ones may need a squeaky wheel (that might be *you*).

Other times, someone was lazy. *Sigh*. A painful reality, but police departments are made of people, and not everyone is a go-getter. Some are even no-getters.

As a cop, this is embarrassing to admit, but I am going to shoot straight with you in this book. The good news is this is not common, and when the bosses find the problem, it's all, "Lucy, you've got some 'splaining to do!" (in my best Desi Arnez voice). OK young grasshopper, if you don't understand the reference, use that newfangled Googles on the Internets.

BE PATIENT

Are you confused yet? I know it can be frustrating to find someone at the station to talk to—especially getting to the *right* one. And while there always could be somebody in a police department that is not exactly "officer friendly" and doesn't help as much as you would like, usually there's simply a little hunting going on to get the right cop. No need to worry; just be patient.

WHAT MAKES A GOOD COP?

OK, it's time to be fair. Since I gave you the rundown about a true crime's intentions, we need to talk about what the ideal intentions of a murder cop *should* be.

This is important—intentions and ethics work both ways. The intentions and motivations found in the best murder cops are the same as those in the list I set out for you, the true crime. A murder cop who isn't a murder cop for the right reasons isn't going to be very good to start with and may be really frustrating to work with, if we can even call it that.

To start with, a murder cop must be hungry. Hungry for the work, responsibility, and accountability. All three of these are equally important. *A murder cop must believe in the mission of finding the truth and following the rules along the way.*

Next, a murder cop must be humble. Death investigation will serve humble pie by the slice, so you might as well have a taste for it. We all know what a lack of humility looks like; arrogance, cockiness, egotism; maybe the Latin word I am looking for is an asshole. People who aren't humble will never be a team player, and their motivations probably are wrong as well.

TV and movies build up the role of the murder cop as walking on the moon in the cop world, and usually, murder cops are portrayed as know-it-alls and a one-person show. Few things are as nasty as a murder cop who is closed-minded, knows it all, and never sees themselves as being wrong.

Murder cops need real people skills. I am not saying they must be an extrovert (I'm an introvert myself), but a murder cop needs sharp communication and social skills. Sure, this helps with interviews, but just as importantly, they've got to be able to build rapport with *EVERYONE* they meet. They need strong relationships with teammates, the bosses, and of course the people they meet in the community they serve.

A murder cop who can't figure out how to get along with other people won't last very long in the business. Cases won't get cleared, and survivors will get more frustrated.

The checklist of virtuous to selfish motivations I gave you works for murder cops as well. As you read this list, watch how motivations move from ideal to egotistical.

A Checklist for Their Intentions

- I value the truth above all else.
- I want to help turn wrongs into rights.
- I am passionate about helping those that are helpless.
- I know what it's like to be a victim and can relate.
- My heart hurts for people lost in pain and darkness.
- I want to be part of something bigger than myself.
- I want to be part of a team that helps others.
- I want my satisfaction to come from within.
- I want to be seen as a hero.
- I want to be famous and for everyone to know me.
- If I can find a big clue, I will be better than everyone else.
- I think most people are bad, and bad people should be punished.
- If I can knock down cases, by any means necessary, I could get promoted.
- It's not so much about the victim's family as it is about me.

Cool. Not only do you know what a good murder cop looks like, but I would say you should go for all the good traits you can pick up from the list.

HOW MURDER COPS BECOME MURDER COPS

Just like you might find a murder cop stationed in different places within a police department, how they get there also varies. There's more than one career path.

Here are some possibilities. Watch and learn because some of these paths may affect the capability of a murder cop in some way.

- **Application, Assessment, and Selection:** Just like it sounds, interested officers hear of an opening, apply, go through testing and an interview or selection process, and the best officer is chosen. Just like your job, aye? This isn't very common in smaller departments, but it is possible. Selection processes are often required in union and collective bargaining contracts—an attempt to create a fair process.

- **Seniority:** In some cases, murder cops are selected based on seniority alone. An opening comes available and the person that has been around the longest gets the gig. This is one of the scariest methods, because it has zero to do with the hunger, humility, and people skills we talked about earlier. In worst case scenarios, the investigations department becomes a retirement home. You can smell the Bengay when you walk into the office, not to mention the mason jars of false teeth on the back of the desks. I'll give you three guesses about what kind of person you might be meeting. In police culture, seniority solves many disputes because the culture thinks using seniority is "fair." Truth be told, more often than not it's easier for leaders to fall on seniority in lieu of making difficult selection decisions based on hunger and skill. I didn't say it was right. It's just the facts, ma'am.

- **Cherry-Picked:** Some murder cops are handpicked by a
  chief or sheriff. It's more common in smaller agencies, but
  even in larger ones chiefs and sheriffs may want to have a
  say on more sensitive or high-dollar assignments. This can
  be a *good* thing. Of course, it could also be a problem if
  people get picked out of favoritism over work ethic,
  experience, and passion. You've seen this hot mess where
  you've worked; you're not alone.

A couple of other factors that might come up—movies and TV
have not helped this—are **rank and pay**.

- **Climbing the Ranks:** In some departments, becoming a
  murder cop (or any detective assignment) is advance in
  rank. Others, not. This can be good or bad. It sort of creates
  a class system between murder cops and patrol officers,
  which in turn can lead to people not getting along and
  sharing information. This is why in some places (including
  movies) the murder cops boss the patrol officers around.
  Trust me, that just doesn't sit well with cops. Even without
  an advancement in rank, the perceived status can be a
  powerful incentive for cops to want to be a murder cop.
  Wave the red flag! This is an extrinsic (outside) motivator;
  it's usually not heart-felt. Like most other extrinsic
  motivations, it's there one minute and gone the next. A cop
  may have some hunger for the position, but if it's hunger
  for power, it's the wrong appetite for this job.

- **Pay:** Taking on the murder cop position sometimes includes
  an increase in pay. Where I spent twenty-eight years as a
  cop, murder cops made the same pay as patrol officers. In
  other places, there may be a pay bump. While that sounds
  fine, the red flag flies because, once again, we're talking
  extrinsic motivation instead of intrinsic motivation. I
  wouldn't want a murder cop working a case close to me that

was only in the job for the money. Would you? Personally, I prefer no pay or rank increases. Being a murder cop should be all about doing it for the right reasons. Just an opinion from an old-school cop, but I am sure tons of cops agree, and certainly many more survivors. I want a murder cop who is doing the job because it speaks to their heart, not their wallet.

By now, you might be asking what this means for you. Just stay with me because you are learning more real stuff than TV has ever shown. I believe there is a place for true crimers to help solve crimes, but if you're going to do that, you've got to do more than just talk to a murder cop, you've got to build a successful relationship with one.

TRAINING

How much training do murder cops get? You guessed it. It depends.

In an ideal world, cops get the best training out there when they take on the role of a murder cop. They get the training before they catch their first case—the most up-to-date training around, learning all of the human and technical skills to become a first-class gumshoe.

Fortunately, this happens in many instances. But not always. None of what I am about to talk about even comes close to saying there is anything like incompetence going on, it's far from that. The experiences a patrol officer goes through are the perfect learning platform for murder cop work, and in virtually every situation, experienced murder cops are there to take newer cops under their wing.

In many police departments, like mine, every officer had to spend at least three years on patrol—the road, as we called it—before they could be considered for *any* specialty assignment like homicide. The time spent on patrol is where cops sharpen their skills, turn experience into wisdom, and in many cases, develop relationships with potential information sources (a.k.a. informants). The busier the police department, the more they will learn.

But make no mistake about it, even with years spent on the road with patrol, the move to homicide is usually a baptism by fire. And as odd as it may sound, it works, and works well.

Some police departments do try to provide specific training and manage to land some fine stuff for the murder cops. A bunch of the training is likely to come after officers become a murder cop because most police departments don't have the luxury of staffing or the time to fully prepare a new detective before they're on the beat. And of course, the practical experience every day and every night are a graduate level education.

Before you get offended, these days the devil is in the money and staffing. Initiatives like "defund the police" can be thanked for that. What gets cut? Training. Staffing. Safety for you and me. Tough stuff with no easy answers.

When training is available, the topics span a wide spectrum, ranging from basic criminal investigation classes to advanced digital forensics. There are schools offering courses in interview and interrogation, crime scene analysis, and more. You name it, it's out there somewhere. There are even classes on working with information sources. (Did you see me look at you when I said that?)

You'll never find a murder cop who is *done* learning. And if you meet one that says they are, or that they've seen it all, good luck! Because that, my friends, is a problem. A humble murder cop, the kind we like, will let people know when they don't know something and look for help. They'll never stop learning.

Don't forget to look for help in your investigations as well. Everyone should always be learning.

THE CASE LOAD: RAKING LEAVES ON A WINDY DAY

Before you write me off as just making excuses, hold up. Just give me a second. The whole point of this book is about helping YOU be a better true crimer. Whether you want to crack a cold case or interview a cop for your show, you're not getting anywhere if you don't understand reality.

Hollywood leaves the impression that police resources are like the all-you-can-eat buffet on a Caribbean cruise. It couldn't be further from the truth. You'd be hard-pressed to find one agency that operates like NCIS.

What do you get when you have cases constantly coming in and fewer people to work them? (Thanks, funding cuts.)

Overrun. Ran over. Beat down. Frustrated. Tired. Burned Out. Just to start… This is the brutal reality wherever you go.

A murder cop's caseload never stops building. Take a vacation? Your inbox is loading up and waiting for you. Off to train for a week? Don't worry. The pile of cases on the corner of your desk will just keep growing—no sunlight or water required.

Most days, a murder cop feels like they are raking leaves on a windy day, and you know what? They are.

I am not telling you this so you can whip out the world's smallest violin, and we can cry together, but this is super important to understand when you want to meet with a murder cop.

Hear this: they use their time *very* carefully and can't stand to waste even a minute of it. One of my first murder mentors (that has an odd sound) gave me the most critical advice my first week in the unit; he said time management is everything, and he was right.

It's like a hospital emergency room. Fifty people might be sitting in the waiting room, and every one of them feels like they need to be seen first. But the doctors can't do that. They can't stitch up a cut and restart someone's heart at the same time. Hence, triage—the staff lines up the patients based on need and takes the most critical cases first.

The biggest impact of triaging in the police world: missing persons cases.

Frightened and frustrated family and friends want their case worked on right away, understandably. They want investigators to leave no stone unturned, as they should. It's not an unreasonable expectation. What they don't realize is that in reality, thousands and thousands of missing persons reports are made every year. There has to be a way of selecting the cases that need the quickest attention because the workload of cases is so demanding. Truth be told, most missing people are not truly *missing*, or at least were never harmed or in danger of being harmed.

Policing is like any business; a budget only has so much money to get you so many people, and that has a direct effect on the work that can be done. Law enforcement doesn't run like Congress and the Federal Reserve; we can't just print more money. (Sorry, I digress.)

Murder cops are usually hired for a 40-hour work week, like most of the work world, and overtime is tightly controlled. As I said, money doesn't grow on trees. But that doesn't mean the cop doesn't care.

Not a day goes by when I don't think about a case that I worked on that has not been laid down. Not a day. There will always be a nagging feeling that if I had more time, if the next case didn't drop in my lap the next week, I could have turned a corner. All murder cops live with this sense of falling short and letting survivors down. Even in the closed cases, the successes where we got the bad guy, I never went to trial feeling like every stone had been turned. There's always more I would have liked to have done. That damn time thing. It's never enough.

Time is the biggest and most legit speed bump you will hit when you hunt down your murder cop. You might only get ONE shot at making an impression with a murder cop, so it needs to be your best. Stay with me and I'll show you how to get your foot in the door and develop a relationship with them. Just don't forget to pack your patience.

THE GOOD, THE BAD, AND THE UGLY

One last tidbit before we move on. This is not easy for a career cop to talk about—but somehow, I need you to get comfortable enough to trust me and what I am saying, and vulnerability is the first step down that path.

Police departments are made up of people. You know, human beings. It's no different than where you've worked; people are people and will never be perfect. And things don't always work the way we would like them to.

Maybe I am making a disclaimer; maybe I want to acknowledge something you may feel. I will always argue that American policing is done exceptionally every day. The bad things, the mistakes, the times when police find crooks among their own ranks, drop the ball on a case, or otherwise let us down, can happen. They do happen. These cases always land in the headlines, but they are the outliers. No matter how cops are being portrayed, the industry does a terrific job every day. Part of the culture we live in tends to treat the exceptions as the rule, and that is simply wrong.

Are there some bad cops out there? Yes, in varying degrees, and the worst, honestly, you don't need to be on the job. True, a small number are truly criminal, corrupt, abusive, etc., but when you see things not done well, it's usually a result of the same thing you see at your job: laziness.

Of course, the stakes are higher in law enforcement and should be, but laziness exists everywhere you go. Unfortunately, some officers (sigh) are not motivated by the right reasons; others are burned out but don't know it yet.

It's important to recognize this because laziness is *not* corruption. Be careful of using words like *corruption* unless corruption is there. I see that word getting tossed around loosely just because people don't agree with where the cops are on a case. Corruption is truly unethical and often illegal behavior.

I'm not making excuses, but every now and then, a problem comes up, and it's usually a specific person. It's rare that these types of folks are in the death investigation business because most homicide investigations get a ton of attention from the public, and the damage to a case and the surviving family could be devastating and heartbreaking. They shouldn't be anywhere. But again, it's actually rare, and the chances of you stumbling across a bad cop are not likely.

You needed to hear me say that, and I needed to tell you.

CHAPTER 6

WHO'S EVERYONE TO EVERYONE ELSE?

OK. WE'VE TALKED about who the true crimers are (and the true crime community). We've talked about the murder cops and how their world operates. We've recognized that, *for the most part,* both groups have the same, well-intended goals. The similarities between them are too familiar to deny: drive, passion, compassion, creativity, imagination, maturity, and an ethical compass. Both sides share these. Why, then, do we see such a rift between the two camps?

The answer is, it's all relative.

It's time to try on one another's shoes for a minute or two.

WHO ARE THE MURDER COPS TO THE TRUE CRIME COMMUNITY?

When it comes to what civilians think of cops, it starts with the five scenarios that form our impressions, perceptions, and expectations.

1. Encounters: The civilian finds themself being "policed." Oof. Encounters with cops can leave lasting impressions, especially if a law has been broken. For most, it's simple: if the cops seemed fair, the memory may not be all that bad, even if someone landed in jail. But, if the cop was an asshole, or worse abusive or lied, than that's a hard place to grow from. Friends of friends who have had bad experiences will usually share the same opinions, even if they didn't witness anything firsthand. This can range from experiences we have in a simple traffic stop to being the focus of a criminal investigation.

Encounters also include the times we are consumers of police services. For example, when we call to submit an accident report, to rat out the neighbor's teenagers throwing a ruckus party, or to report a crime, any situation where we seek help from the police. For a lot of young people today, this may start with the officers on detail to protect your school. Back in the '80s and '90s, a lot of us met officers through Drug Abuse Resistance Education (DARE) programs.

Regardless of the situation, if the cop we get is professional, caring, and interested in helping us, we leave with a pretty good opinion of cops.

On the other hand, if the cop is rude, impatient, or dismissive, we will usually have a low opinion of who cops are. It's no different than any other customer service we might receive in the food or retail industries.

2. Hollywood and TV: If anything (other than the cops themselves) has worked harder than the media to derail trust with cops, I'd like to see it. Think about all of the movies and TV shows you've seen. I bet you can count on one hand how many painted the police in something close to respectable.

This, of course, multiplies today with the ease of independent movie and film making, where flat-out anti-police agendas are prolific. If the person watching these videos lacks a few critical thinking skills and fills up their tank of confirming evidence bias with them, imagine the result? The good cops don't stand a chance.

If your impressions about police are formed from movies and TV, it might be time to put down the popcorn bucket and step away from the screen. More than likely, you paid too damn much for the popcorn anyway.

3. Generational Hand-Me-Downs: This one has real legs, in my opinion. In cases where bad or corrupt policing targeted groups of people, for example, people of color or those who are economically challenged, for any length of time, the distrust is handed down from generation to generation. Perceptions and expectations remain even when relationships between the police and community have generally improved. Most American police officers deal with this every day, especially in urban areas.

This is a situation where perception is the reality.

4. Personal Connection: Friends and family members of law enforcement personnel can be some of the most trusting and supportive. Why? They have a personal connection. Their experience with the cop outside of work informs and supports their trust and belief in them on the job. They have a front row seat to the show. They hear the "why" and the "how" more than just the "who, what, and when." They see the long hours and put up with the distraction when a case comes home. And they live with the reality that any "Have a good day at work!" might be their last.

True crimers who've lived up close and personal with a cop get the drift; their expectations show it.

5. Embedded Believers: No, we're not talking about planted informants. We are talking about intentional partnerships designed to bridge the gap between the community and the cops.

In the early '90s, Community Oriented Policing (COP) programs started to make their way into the law enforcement industry. COP was (and still is) a push to respond to crime and quality life issues in a proactive manner, with a focus on community involvement and engagement. This was the start of moving police departments from simply reacting to crime, where it can look more like an occupying force, to servicing the people in the community.

The goals also included getting closer to the people in the community, sort of the "officer friendly" thing, but in a genuine way. Programs popped up like Citizen Police Academies (CPA), where community members were invited to learn the deep details of how police departments work; Citizen Police Academy Alumni Associations (CPAAA), for people to join and stay involved after completing the Citizen Police Academy; and Police Athletic Leagues (PAL), programs that engage local youth in sports and academic development and competition. Many agencies developed community meeting programs, began bicycle and traditional foot patrols in neighborhoods, and invited community members to take part in problem-solving and crime prevention plans, just to name a few.

As skeptical as old-school police might have been of this approach, in many cases, it started to work. Dialogue and transparency increased, and trust between the cops and citizens improved. Go figure.

We tend to trust people who let us get to know them, and vice versa. It's been my experience that once people get embedded in a police department, they feel like they are part of the family. They become more patient with the police, even after critical incidents like a high-profile use of police force.

Here's the deal. A person's experiences with the police create their beliefs of who the police and murder cops are—good, bad, or indifferent. The goal is to move toward good experiences and perceptions. It ain't gonna happen overnight; it'll take continual work from *both* the community *and* the police.

WHO IS THE TRUE CRIME COMMUNITY TO THE MURDER COPS?

Let's flip this coin and look at the other side. Who are citizens to the police, and what role do they play? More to the point, how do the cops view the true crimer?

First off, the citizens in the community are the customers to the police; the reason they exist in the first place. (At least in the US.) The police look out for the citizens, sort of like a guard dog over a gentle herd of animals, protecting everyone from the wolf stalking just a few feet away.

That may sound idealistic and lofty, especially in these first few years of the 2020s, but it's true. I mentioned earlier that there are bad cops out there, but in 28 years of service, I can count on one hand how many cops I knew of who didn't belong on the job. But it stops there.

That said, several things affect the cop's attitude in the community. Sometimes it shows, sometimes it doesn't. More often than not, their attitudes come with a reason.

First off, *EVERYONE* lies.

Well, not *everyone*, but to be a cop is to dive into a deep pool of lies, deception, and manipulation. They spend their days dealing with the dark side. Funny thing, crooks and criminals don't like to get caught. Who'd have guessed that? Ask any police officer and they will tell you that hearing the truth, large or small, is rare. *So* rare, they stay skeptical even with proof.

This is big, so don't gloss over it.

Now, who are you, dear community citizen? You are an information source.

That's it. Straight up. I didn't say informant, or confidential informant (a CI as we say), although you could be. Those names are too specific right now. I am sorry if it felt glamorous for a second.

For the police, information sources come in many shapes and sizes. You and your motivation will figure out where you fit, but until the copper gets a clear idea of why you are offering help, they will wonder —and likely be distrustful. Hopefully, politely distrustful.

It's a thing. I was good at not tipping anyone off to my reticent curiosity in a way that might offend.

Based on the honesty circus—remember, we deal with bad guys— cops are trained to be skeptical. Sometimes that gets misunderstood, but we are talking about a group of people that have an incredible amount of authority: they can seize (take) things (property). They can seize (take) people. As in, take another person's freedom. And based on our social contract and law, they can literally take someone's life in the most desperate situations. Do you want them taking *your* freedom based on a false report? I didn't think so.

Chances are, you might not have ever thought about them that way. Of course, there is a mountain of responsibility and accountability that goes along with all of this. They never want to get ANY of this wrong. Before they exercise that authority, they better be damn sure the information they have is right.

That's why whenever anyone offers up information, or shows an interest in an incident or investigation, the antenna goes up and the radar turns on.

Earlier, I talked about your intentions as a member of the true crime community. Let's dive a little deeper for a minute and look at those motivations from the viewpoint of the murder cop, because your motivation is one of the first things a murder cop will be trying to figure out. It plays a big role in how they evaluate what you are offering, and of course, how truthful they think you are.

Cops are trained in reading people, and they sharpen their skills with time and experience. They'll be quietly evaluating the information you offer, as well as how truthful they think you are. They'll also be comparing it to the motivations they uncover in anyone else who shows up as a potential source of information.

Sometimes, the cop will ask you directly why you are coming forward. I really recommend telling the truth—like I said, they'll be skeptical until they see it for themselves. If it turns out you weren't telling the truth, they will be done with you. In some cases, you could also face real legal trouble.

There are five reasons people supply information to the law. Each one of these carry risks for the murder cop; even the most seemingly commendable can be risky. All of them are driven by emotion in some way, and emotions often blur the vision of even the most well-intentioned people.

1. The Honest and Concerned Citizen (No, Not a Karen): This is the person who offers information simply because it's the right thing to do, because they care about people as a whole. They have a strong moral and ethical compass and a conscience that will not rest if they don't speak up. These folks likely believe that they have a responsibility as a citizen to take an active role if they can do so.

Our communities would look totally different if more people were motivated like this. The sad truth is they are rare, so rare that murder cops will start out skeptically waiting for the shoe to drop because it's just too good to be true.

Once a cop figures out this is real, a powerful relationship is born. Founded on mutual respect and admiration, it might even last years, extending well beyond the case work. How do I know this? Because my co-workers and I saw this often enough to believe people like this are still out there.

Don't be fooled, these people come from every walk of life. Some of the most outstanding humans I came to know were people the rest of the community looked down on. Drug addicts, prostitutes, thieves; you name it. While they fought demons of their own, they still knew right from wrong.

Some people even come forward with information on family and friends, simply because it is the right thing to do. Wow. Think about how hard that is to do. Could you do that?

If this is who you are, you are incredible and commendable. If you are not there all the way, that's OK. Just don't bullshit your way there. Be patient with the law as they figure you out; if you do, you can find yourself in with the A-Team.

2. The Karen: Oh, snap! There is a Karen after all! Ya don't say. (Sorry if your name is Karen. But your parents did that, not me. Be a Karen and take it up with them.)

The Karen is relatively new, thanks to social media. But some information sources are just that. There are people who report things to *look* like they are concerned and honest citizens. The truth is, they just like being in other people's shit.

Sure, *some* of the things they report can be good information to work with, but like I said and will keep saying, the motivation is sketchy. A cop's bullshit meter reads endless frequencies and spectrums, and it's perfectly calibrated for is what we now lovingly call "The Karen."

For a patrol officer—where honestly, cops get the most info—these are the nosy or spiteful neighbors who call in with exaggerated stuff:

The child that is left alone in the house for *days*... that the cops find out is a really smart fourteen-year-old latchkey kid.

The ball in the yard from the kids next door.

The trash cans left out front the day after pick-up. (The absolute horror!)

Here is one from my town. Follow me, it's true.

According to city rules, you could only water on particular days of the week during a drought. During a dry spell, we'd get a barrage of neighbors dialing 9-1-1 to rat old Ben for watering on Wednesday. Or sweet Georgia, who dared turn her garden hose on for her roses on Thursday.

If neighbors ratted out neighbors over violent crime like they did over water ban violations, we would live in utopia! No kidding. I could have an illegal marijuana grow with 1,000 plants in the backyard, and the cops would never be told. But if I watered my tomatoes on Tuesday instead of Wednesday, I'm off to life in Sing Sing for hard labor with no shot at parole.

You see the problem. And as you investigate a case, you will really see the problem. Don't be a Karen. Treat the Karens you meet kindly, but hold them at a distance that they don't see.

3. Let's Get Even (Because Who Wins with Odd): Ah, revenge! It's so delicious when served up steaming hot.

People who want to get back at someone else *love* to dime people out. Someone who was once a confidant will march into court and bury you. There are more of these than virtuous informants, trust me.

Have you ever heard the saying, "Hell hath no fury like a woman scorned"? I have dropped cases on that very gig! Pro tip: never tell your special partner about doing bad things, like murder and rape. If you do, keep them happy and never leave them. You, my friend, are welcome.

This is common, and obviously, it can work in the cop's favor. However, the problem for a murder cop is that this information is not being offered for the good—it's every bit emotional, and emotions are roadblocks in looking for the truth.

When emotions get hijacked, people get blinded. We don't think things through; it's easy to exaggerate details. In most cases, we don't want to listen to any side other than our own and only look for stuff that fits our argument. So, clearly, honesty may not be onboard.

Lastly, a big problem with the reliability of this information source is that folks kiss and make up. Suddenly, everything is different. Keep in mind, we are typically talking about whatever information was brought forward, going to court, and getting a witness to testify. You don't have to watch all the crime shows out there to get why this information isn't taken to heart until it's independently corroborated.

Talk about having the rug pulled out from under your feet. For a cop, it has little to do with feeling disappointed and everything to do with watching justice walk away.

If this is you, and you come forward and it helps a case, thanks. But don't expect to be invited to the homicide office Christmas party.

4. Let's Make a Deal! (I'd Gladly Pay You Tuesday for a Hamburger Today) OK, Monty Hall! Let's make a deal! If there was a star rating for a criminal's defense strategy—as in, what's the least punishment I can get for this shit—winner, winner chicken dinner! Making a deal earns an automatic six on a 5-star scale.

If there is ever a place for balance in the community of cops, prosecutors, crime victims, and survivors, here it is.

Deals are part of the criminal justice system. The most common comes in the form of a plea bargain: a defendant (no longer just a suspect) agrees to admit to committing certain crimes or actions in return for a reduced or lighter sentence. This is usually very frustrating —unless you are a suspect. Then, of course, life is good. Well, maybe not good, but you get the point.

Sometimes deals are made in exchange for information that looks like it will move a case forward (in this case the snitches could get stitches, but reduced time as well). Sometimes a case that starts out promising for the prosecution gets shaky (witnesses can't be found or change their testimony, evidence or statements are suppressed by the court, or victims become reluctant to participate in the process), and deals get dealt.

Many deals are made in court. Which, as frustrating as it is, keeps the justice system from crawling to a halt. And, in that deal-making, there is a sense of discretion, grace, and procedural justice. For court deals, the big consideration is how the crime victim (or survivors) feels about the deal that is going to be offered. At least it should be that way. Sadly, sometimes these deals are cut without talking to the people who lived through the crime. This usually pisses the cops off, as well.

As far as these deal makers being witnesses, they are low on the trust poll. A considerable amount of work will go into corroborating anything they offer. A primary rule for cops and prosecutors is that no case should ever rest on this type of information; the case has to stand on its own without the deal taker's help. That is how untrustworthy this stuff is.

What part of makin' a deal applies to you and me?

Murder cops frequently have people approach them with an offer of information in order to help themselves or someone they know in a jam. For obvious reasons, cops tread lightly here. The balancing act is simple: how does the information offered look against the crimes and punishments they are trying to avoid? Sort of like risk and reward.

The first rule of thumb is that we don't deal with violent offenders or any other serious offense. But that is not a hard rule. In extreme cases, people who murder can use their cooperation, but they have to super-size their info and give up other *really* bad people, or bodies.

Narcotics detectives live by this. Pinch a person selling dope and they'll roll right over. They don't want to be in trouble, so they give up someone higher in the dealing system. The detectives wire up (covert listening or recording devices) and send the suspect to make a dope purchase, sometimes even from a friend. That's some kind of friend! The real wins are when the suspect offers information on bigger cases, like a murder.

Sometimes the deals are smaller and quicker. For me, it was not uncommon to have a source approach me and say they had a misde-meanor warrant (in other words, they were on the "let's go to jail" party list). If the informant was working for me, I'd go see a judge and ask that the warrant be changed to a summons (no jail). I never had a judge turn me down. But to be clear, I *never* did this in cases where their standing charges involved violence or risked putting anyone in danger.

I never fully trusted any of these informants; I got burned a few times. But the risk was always low, and working murder cases always involves some careful risk.

One time, I got a dude out of jail who assured me he could buy a murder gun for one of my cases. When we talked, I reminded him that if he ducked out on me, the prosecutor would make an open record in court as to what he was supposed to do, and a warrant would be issued.

He popped smoke. We went to court with a room full of people, mostly defendants (some in jumpsuits), and the prosecutor told the judge exactly what had happened. You could have heard a pin drop. I would not want to be that guy in the criminal community.

Working with dealmakers means hitting mostly dead ends and getting lied to, but you still work this magic because when it pays off, it pays off big! And a victim deserves every bit of the effort.

5. The Supplemental Income Generator (a.k.a. the Secret Side Hustle): Yep. Many people who bring information to police do so for the cold, hard cash. Flat out, this informant is all about making some money. I knew several people who used this as a pretty good side hustle for years, and no one ever knew they were snitching. You see, maybe it's true when they say, "snitches get stitches," but it's also true that "snitches get riches."

The amount of money can vary and can come from different sources. The most common ones we see are the rewards offered by police or families. I said 'offered' because, in the real world, these don't pay out as often as we would like. I would never write them off as not working, or not worth the time, but it's one of those things where your expectations have to be real.

Trading dollars for details also includes programs like Crime Stoppers. I am a huge fan of Crime Stoppers; in many places, they work really well. Crime Stoppers contracts with a local media outlet, like a TV station, to produce awareness shows and invite John Q. Public to call in and anonymously report a tip. If the scoop gets something done, the tipster is paid confidentiality. A bunch of crimes get solved by Crime Stoppers, and many more wanted people get caught—all because people tip the law.

Yet another money maker for your shaker is the real-deal police informant. This is super sexy stuff right here, folks.

The confidential informant (the mysterious "CI"), the paid informant, the qualified informant—there are tons of names for these cats. Now, any one of them, and it's really the norm, might be motivated by any of the things we already talked about. But when murder cops want to have a source at this level, a whole lot of work goes into validating their potential honesty, value, and reliability. There is a pretty good load of paperwork and documentation that is kept under tight wraps. So tight, only a few other cops in an agency can even go into the room where the records are kept—most don't even know the room exists, let alone where it is.

Why? Because if these info sources are reliable and productive, their lives are literally at risk. Sure, case work can be damaged, but the primary concern is for the informant's safety.

Record keeping is significant outside of the secret squirrel room, as well. A proven and reliable informant can actually remain anonymous in arrest and search warrant affidavits (that's the thingy that cops write to show a judge they have probable cause) and courtroom procedures. No shit! They can hide out pretty much all the way up to direct testimony as a full-blown witness.

Tidbit time: most cops will work informants just up to needing them to testify, because once they testify, they'll be exposed (obviously). Not to worry. The murder cops just need independent corroboration of the key facts, and all is right with the community.

Some of my bravest, contributing community members were in this group. That said, I really don't think a true crimer should enter the world of the CI. Here's why.

First, it's all about reliability and has little to do with the informant's character and overall honesty. These people typically live in the criminal community, and, sad to say, reliability is limited to documented tasks and events, no more.

Working with a CI really has little to do with a cop actually trusting the informant. It's more about patterns of behavior, good or bad. CIs that produce and are reliable get work; those that are not reliable, don't.

Second, there are no lifetime memberships in this club. Literally one snafu—not even big—and the cops disqualify informants immediately. They alert their prosecutors and literally flag their names for life in the CI files. That way, another cop doesn't unknowingly re-enlist the informant into the ranks of a secret crime fighter, even years down the road.

Third, because there is no trust, there is nothing that resembles a relationship. Cops are trained to stay at a distance, and most police policy bans anything friendly or close to it. Nada. Zip. Nothin'. The informant is kept at a strict distance, and the best cops never let an informant forget it. Stepping across that line will not only end in a disappointed cop, but maybe, in the worst cases, an unemployed cop or a cop in prison.

If you're an authentic true crimer, I highly doubt you're going to be satisfied working on the pay-to-play plan.

One Word: Why?

At the end of the day, how do we know how someone is motivated?

Did you see yourself in any of these profiles? I really hope you fall into the ideally motivated categories. It's just as important to consider motivations of those we follow or get involved with. Heck, even before you share that TikTok post. Do you want your name associated with some shifty, self-serving "influencer"?

I am a big fan of simply asking, "Why?" In most cases, folks won't use the exact words I did above, but now that you have an inside scoop, you'll pick up on what's motivating them to make their claims. After all, you get to choose who you hitch your wagon to.

Here's my point. I want you to enjoy the world of true crime by being deeply immersed in the game. This includes everything from being an interested bystander and simply watching and listening, to getting involved as an amateur detective and working on a case. Use this insight to help you become a respected information source with a murder cop. Use it to build trust. Stop playing on the edge, always negotiating and wondering where you stand, and get in the middle of the game.

I honestly want your heart and work to be recognized and rewarded. You can make a difference in cases.

PART TWO
THE MINEFIELD

CHAPTER 7
WHEN WORLDS COLLIDE

DOES the true crime community help or hurt cases?

The answer is: *Yes*. It does both, and the pendulum swings wide depending on each case.

We watch a lot of true crime programs in our house. That's all my wife Wendy ever has on TV, whether I choose it or not! I tend to favor programs that are more authentic and fact-based than those that simply gloss over the story or delve into weird conspiracy theories. There are many shows I respect greatly—they clearly put a great deal of care into the production.

Some shows are good, some are very bad. And then there is a third category that can only be described accurately as *stupid*.

At their worst, true crimers can cause cases to fall apart, tampering with evidence and destroying venues for a fair trial. They might get their downloads, but in the end, justice dies. I get it; some people don't know any better. No shit, Sherlock! But when we don't know, then we should pipe down a bit until we do.

If we agree we all want the truth—and the justice that may follow —we've got to find a way to do this better. Most of the problems come down to a lack of understanding the process and poor communication.

Part 2 of this book is here so you don't look stupid.

TYPES OF INVESTIGATORS

There are four types of true crime investigators. While roles and motivations might impact this, it's not quite the same. Investigators are
active (not just curious). Their type has more to do with results than
intentions.

First, the well-intentioned, naive crowd. Here we are, paving that
damn road to hell again.

Next, there are those who stomp around without caring and blow
things up, almost as if on purpose.

Then, there's a mix of both—the folks who dive into the true crime
world but are both naive and so burdened with biases that they end up
being the bull in the China shop—or, in this case, the heavy foot stepping on mines everywhere they walk.

All three of these types end up with the same reckless results. If we
really care about survivors and justice, we don't want to be that person.
I hope none of you want to be *that* person.

That leaves us with the fourth type: the thoughtful investigator.

This person has an honest head on their shoulders, driven by
virtuous intentions. They're aware they don't know it all, but they're
eager to listen and learn. They might step on a mine or two (we all do
at some point; it's called learning), but they're willing to own it, learn
from it, and keep pressing on to help others.

Here's the deal. Investigating a case really doesn't require a formal
head nod saying it's your job. It does require a sense of curiosity,
driven by virtuous intentions (serious here), and an ability to recognize
personal biases with a strong enough will to check powerful emotions.
Whether you're a murder cop or a true crimer, we need to check our
emotions and not let the emotions of other people hijack ours.

There are countless examples of how people who never took an
oath have done spectacular work and moved cases forward, solved
mysteries, and helped deliver justice. This, by the way, also includes
exoneration, which is just as important.

WORKING TOGETHER

So, how do we get everyone on the same page and close some cases? Like so many things in life, two people can share motivation, passion, and vision for the same destination but pass like two ships in the night —or worse—collide.

Let's all agree that the true crime community is full of potential for helping solve cases. You've got time, the ability to pool people to think creatively and gather information, and the desire to get justice for survivors. Fantastic.

Murder cops know how to work the cases in order to get them into the criminal justice system. Let's go!

If you understand the process, you can do this thoughtfully. But you've got to know how to watch your step—it's time to head into the minefield of investigations.

CHAPTER 8

THE MINEFIELD: WATCH WHERE YOU STEP

NAVIGATING THE INVESTIGATION MINEFIELD

THE BUSINESS of criminal investigations can be a minefield. Any of us can walk into this amazing world armed with the best of intentions and start puttering around in what looks like a soft pasture on a beautiful day. Then, BOOM! We accidentally step on something that puts us, other people, and an investigation in harm's way.

I'm going to help you identify the most common land mines. Here's a hint: they are rarely in plain view. You've got to know what you're looking for and where to look.

This is nothing new for the murder cops. These charges and trip-wires are everywhere we turn; part of sharpening our saw is learning how to navigate around or avoid them.

Some of these will not affect the true crimer directly—at least not to the same extent as murder cops (because you are not the government)—but you could step close enough to put a case at risk, and in turn, cause pain in the life of a survivor. Besides that, it never hurts to get a deeper understanding as to why things are or aren't done in murder investigations or why they take as long as they do.

We will start on what sounds like the negative side, but as you read,

I will move into tips for understanding investigations or really helping cases, should you decide to get involved.

My intention and motivation: I want to protect any survivors, the victim's family, and my new friend in true crime, you.

One important tidbit. Everything I talk about will be in general terms. *I am not giving legal instruction or advice*. The land mines are sitting in a field made up of our Constitution, local laws (including city, county, state, or tribal laws), as well as years of court decisions and appeals. It's incredibly complex. If you get on this field to play, it's up to you to know the details of the laws that apply.

In Judge Harold J. Rothwax's book *Guilty: The Collapse of Criminal Justice*, he opines that all of this is *too* complex, citing that if a cop locked him or herself away in a library for six months to read every law and nuisance, they'd still struggle once back into the real world. Great book, by the way. Read it (once you are done reading this book, of course).

If, at any point, you aren't sure where you're going or where the danger is, stop. Stop and think. No harm in that. You can learn more, regroup, and move again, but there is no shame in your game if you stop. Murder cops stop all the time, so can you.

Now, let's talk about each land mine.

#1 THE HOUSE OF PAIN

Never add to the pain of a murder victim's survivors. Ever.
Murder cops exist to find and record the truth as advocates for the victims, the survivors, and, in turn, society. Avoiding causing pain is like trying to navigate a minefield because a murder cop must step carefully through an ugly world of abrupt and painful truths and realities yet somehow keep the emotional well-being of the survivors balanced as much as possible. Certainly, a good murder cop will have a great deal of social intelligence and compassion. They realize they may be the last string of hope for the survivors, and they do their best not to

cause more pain than the survivor is already suffering. This must hold true for everyone in the police business.

This can still go wrong in the murder biz. Take a look at these scenarios:

Ego over service: If a detective is there to feed his or her own ego, they will never have enough empathy and sympathy for the survivors —and it will show. They will be arrogant, aloof, and callous, lacking patience or a servant attitude. This will leave survivors in the dark. I'd add they suck anyway; ego and investigations never mix.

Victim blaming: Man, this is a tough one for a murder cop. Murder investigations, whether solved in 30 minutes or 30 years, will focus on victimology. This is really no more than a deep dive into who the victim was, as deep as possible. It's where cases can gain solvability factors. It can be a landmine, though, because we are looking for risk factors: what was going on with the victim or around the victim that could have played a role in their murder?

For a survivor, this can look insensitive and intrusive—even damning and blaming. We have to handle looking into the victim with care. If there are risk factors we don't know about, the case will drag on, and precious time will be lost. It's hard to stand beside a mother or father that just learned their twenty-seven-year-old son was involved in things they never imagined. Even if they had known, tragedy was never something they imagined for their future. Murder cops let them know we still see him as their son, living in a world where none of us are perfect, and no one gets to take another's life, no matter how the person is living.

Guessing: A murder cop should never, ever, ever fill a survivor's head and heart with lists of personal guesses and assumptions. Even if the theories have legs (workable), these things that sound comforting become informal promises and hope for the survivor. It could be a false hope, though, and if it doesn't play out, it causes pain. I heard a survivor in an unsolved case say that the first detective assured her that there would be an arrest within six months—five years ago and counting.

Being indirect: Bad news is bad news, and nothing changes that. The old spoonful of sugar isn't going to help the medicine go down any easier. In fact, it may backfire and leave a survivor with more questions than answers. Delivering hard news requires patience and trust. We don't want to be cruel, but we do need to be honest. The conversation comes from the murder cops' heart, by putting themselves in the shoes of the survivor. While we may not share every detail of an investigation, when we do, we must be accurate. If we sugar coat a detail and the survivor later learns something different (the truth), we are liars.

Feeding the beast: Survivors in pain have little left but questions, fears, and anxiety. They may not be getting every single detail from the cops, for all the right reasons. The murder cops have asked them not to share the information they have been given. Their family and friends have their own ideas, theories, or suspicions about what happened. And they'll talk about it. The media and the true crime community have ten times that many theories!

These all feed the beast: the survivor's imagination and confusion. It's a beast that has a hunger that's never satisfied. It's always wanting more, and if it smells or hears something appetizing, it'll run it down and feed on that too. Just like being indirect, if the cop doesn't check the survivor's beast with clear facts and logic, the survivor's pain is likely to grow.

Blow the case: If the murder cop does lazy or shoddy work, or isn't skilled in the minefield, the case gets blown. In the United States, we get one bite at the apple because of our prohibition of double jeopardy (trying someone twice for the same crime). I can tell you from experience, it's hard enough for a survivor to watch pre-trial decisions that scare them, or skilled defense attorneys pick a case apart—it's got to be devasting to watch justice fly out the window.

WHAT'S THIS MEAN FOR YOU?

If the murder cops can get this wrong, the true crime community can, too. No matter how you get in the game, everyone needs to live responsibly—especially in this world of instant information.
How can true crimers add pain to somebody already in the most pain they will likely experience in their life?

Here are four ways:

1. **Blow the case:** Mislead the murder cops with unfounded theories or meddling. Drive witnesses and suspects underground. Tamper with evidence. Share case information that should not be shared. Just to name a few. This isn't a playground for entertainment; it's real life, where real people can get hurt. Imagine being the person called out for messing a case up. Then, imagine how the survivors will view you. What would you say to a survivor if your actions screwed a case up and let the bad guy go?

2. **Guessing (out loud):** Don't mistake me on this, one of the cool things about the true crime community is getting together with like-minded folks and trying to figure out what happened. The problem comes if the guessing gets loud and public, and starts to offend the survivors, witnesses, family members, and even potential suspects. We live in the premier land of free speech, but that doesn't mean it doesn't have consequences. Before you speak out loud, think about how it may affect other people and the justice system.

3. **Feeding the beast:** I told you how the murder cops avoid this, but unfortunately, this is the specialty of some people

in the true crime community. Like your imagination and mine, the scenarios the beast can conjure up may not be realistic. In fact, the details imagined could be impossible. The hungry beast lies a lot. He'll make the impossible sound very realistic and gives something like a pseudo-answer to the survivor. The survivor needs facts and objectivity. Occasionally, they need to be confronted bluntly with harsh truths and clarity. What they don't need is for us to feed the beast. I am passionate about this one. Sorry, not sorry. I've seen true crimers who are practically parasitic when it comes to adding confusion and feeding off it, for what can only be selfish reasons. For example, I follow a woman on social media who lost her adult daughter—the death was ruled a suicide. To say she has struggled with the loss is an understatement. She and many around her have had a hard time accepting it as a suicide. Could there be foul play? Possible, but not probable looking at the details she offers. The beast certainly doesn't let her consider suicide. Some do-gooders found her and attached themselves to the cause. Pretty soon, they shared videos of themselves protesting at a police department, yelling at patrol officers (who would have no knowledge of the case), and posting reels and videos of themselves supposedly anguished with pain and disbelief. No facts. No evidence. Just emotion. The best I could describe it: sickening. Then they moved on to the next beast to feed. What the hell was that? Pain. All I am asking is that if the murder cops have explained things to the survivor, let's keep our opinions and theories to ourselves for the moment. The chances that the cops are lying to the survivor are almost non-existent (I know the haters won't accept that, but oh well). Something as simple as reminding a survivor that the murder cops are the ones with the real facts, may be a better way to keep pain from sharpening.

4. **Blame and shame:** Want to really inflict pain on a
   survivor? Get in the business of blame and shame. There
   are true crimers that seem to take this route before anything
   else. They blame the victim, the victim's family, the friends
   (survivors), decisions, life choices, life struggles, the way
   they look, the way they talk, you name it—good old-
   fashioned victim blaming. Blast that on the internet and it's
   likely to make it back to the people already struggling with
   grief and loss. The only thing that might be more fun than
   blaming is shaming. Sometimes, I think the whole purpose
   of the internet for some folks is to shame others. They get
   the party started by blaming people that have nothing to do
   with the case (other than their opinion) and shame the shit
   out of them. Makes a person feel superior. They were just
   getting started. Next round is called, "Let's go after the
   family of the person we are blaming and get to shaming
   there!" It doesn't matter what they did or didn't do, who
   they did or didn't know, or if we might be jamming up a
   case. Go get 'em! And while we're at it, damn! Let's blame
   those cops! They might not have committed the murder (or
   did they?), but they haven't solved it and won't listen to me,
   so let's have at them too. That's the true crime static that
   amplifies pain—it's what you get when crummy intentions
   take hold in the true crime community. Shameful.

#2 THE CONSTITUTION AND OUR BILL OF RIGHTS

If I had a dollar for every time I heard one of these… I'd be sipping
bourbon on my own private beach.

> *"Why don't they just drag the suspect downtown and make 'em
> talk?!"*

> *"They should have searched them and the house the first time
> they saw them!"*

"They were right there with her and didn't lock her up?"

"EVERYBODY knows he's guilty, but the cops won't arrest him!

"They didn't read me my rights!"

"Can you believe this? She killed that baby and had the cojones to plead NOT GUILTY at her preliminary hearing!!!"

Welcome to the frustration versus reality circus. I understand that frustrated, scared, or hurting people struggle when things are uncertain and answers aren't coming. But most of these statements and questions are the result of Americans who don't have a clue about civics, government, and that magical thing that separates the United States from most of the world: the Constitution and our Bill of Rights.

I am somewhere between perplexed and saddened by people's lack of knowledge or understanding of the Constitution. Is that not taught in school anymore? I have my doubts.

If I sound snarky, it's because I am. These are often the same armchair quarterbacks that pick apart investigations performed by amazing cops. Oh, they know how to cry, "Free speech!" but apparently, they've forgotten that it isn't the only protected right—or that the liberties apply to *everyone*.

I don't expect John Q. Public or the rest of the true crime community to know all the ins and outs of case law, appellate decisions, and the like. But the fundamentals are a different story.

I am not going to conduct a class on the Bill of Rights today, but I'd like to touch on some points that cause confusion.

First and foremost, law enforcement is sworn to uphold and work within the liberties and restrictions of the Bill of Rights. That makes the United States Constitution our coloring book—it defines the lines we have to stay in.

On top of that, countless court cases and appellate decision have further defined what law enforcement (and the government at large) can and cannot do. It's a huge minefield of potential danger in and of itself.

That said, this truly brilliant and timeless document is what separates us from other countries. It is what protects us all; just read the Bill of Rights for yourself. You can. You should. Heck, I even put a copy in the back of this book. For now, let's not dive into a rabbit hole of details. Let's start with three handy definitions of terms that set the bar for when cops *can* and *can't* do something, or how much proof is needed:

- ***Reasonable Suspicion:*** Reasonable suspicion is a term used to describe if a person has been, or will be, involved in a crime based on specific facts and circumstances. It may be used to justify an investigatory stop. (Cue the lights and siren, please.) Reasonable suspicion is more than a hunch that a crime has been committed, but it does not require as much evidence as probable cause—which is needed to obtain search and arrest warrants. We refer to these as Terry stops, from the court case Terry v. Ohio (1968) which ruled an officer can perform a frisk (pat down) of a person during a Terry stop if the officer reasonably believes the person may be armed with a weapon.
- ***Probable Cause:*** Probable cause is defined as a reasonable belief that an individual has, is, or will commit a crime. This belief must be based on facts—not a hunch or suspicion. In order to determine if there was probable cause, the court must find that a person with reasonable intelligence would believe that a crime was being committed under the same circumstances. Probable cause requires stronger evidence than reasonable suspicion.
- ***Proof Beyond a Reasonable Doubt:*** This is defined as any doubt, especially about the guilt of a criminal defendant, that arises or remains upon fair and thorough consideration of the evidence or lack thereof. It's the prosecution's job to bring evidence that gives proof beyond a reasonable doubt.

In the United States, you're still innocent until proven
guilty.

Let's break down some of the questions and statements from above.

"WHY DON'T THEY JUST DRAG THE SUSPECT DOWNTOWN AND MAKE 'EM TALK?!"

A two-part answer. First, the snarky answer is that because this is the United States of America, not some dictator-ruled shell of a foreign country where the rules are made up along the way. Let's start with the basics.

"Dragging" someone away is prohibited by the Fourth Amendment and its protection for all of us that the government cannot "seize" us without probable cause. What that means is that even if the murder cops are 100% sure you are the perp, they cannot simply go out one day, grab you off the street, and take you somewhere else—or for that matter, hold you against your will. They must have probable cause and be able to defend it.

There are the finer matters of reasonable suspicion and Terry stops, but that is a very temporary detention. Even during a Terry stop you only have to identify yourself and don't have to answer *any* questions. If the cops have probable cause or an arrest warrant (obtained with probable cause), they can haul your ass off, no problem.

Now, if the murder cop doesn't have probable cause, all is not lost. Anyone can accept an invitation by the police to talk, just as easily as they can decline an invitation to talk. And that little convo can happen anywhere the person being interviewed agrees to participate.

Many people will "go downtown" with the cops and knock out an interview. If they do, it's because the cops have built a rapport with them, and they feel comfortable taking part in the interview. Innocent and guilty alike will go along with the program.

Now for the second part of the answer. The United States government, as bound by the Bill of Rights, doesn't make people talk. We are blessed to live in a country where the government, primarily by virtue of the Fifth Amendment, cannot make you incriminate yourself. Period.

Cops, murder cops, prosecutors, and judges cannot *drag* you in and we can't *make* you talk. We, as police, can *ask* you to take part in an interview, but you have the right, as Nancy Reagan said, to "just say no." Oh my, some of you may have to Google that one.

Let me reiterate: this doesn't mean people can't speak to the police, and if we gain rapport and trust, we might get someone to cooperate and have a conversation. I hate the word *interrogation*, even though it's the appropriate legal mumbo jumbo for what happens in particular cases. I prefer words like interviews, conversations, and dialogue, because if we are looking for the truth, a respectful chat is the best place to look.

"THEY SHOULD HAVE SEARCHED THEM AND THE HOUSE THE FIRST TIME THEY SAW THEM!"

I hate to come off as sarcastic, but "see above."

That's an oversimplification, so let's go a little deeper. True enough, the Constitution covers the biggest part of this, but I want to carry that into the nuances that the real world brings. Probable cause is a big deal. When you read the definition, it looks cut-and-dried but it's far from it.

There are two challenges cops deal with: the perception of what outsiders see, and what they saw and heard in the moment. In other words, the armchair quarterbacks vs. the people on the field during the game. Hindsight is always 20/20. Reality is played out in the fog somewhere. It comes on a case by case basis.

Searching places and things requires probable cause, an emergency, or consent. The police (government) must follow a strict set of rules when places are searched. Most often, searches of homes, businesses, and the like, will be done with a warrant, approved by a judge after a cop swears to the accuracy of their probable cause on an affidavit for a search warrant.

There are limited circumstances that allow options for sweeping a place for potentially injured people or suspects, but these are rare. There's also consent. The cops can search a place if the people owning or occupying the premise give consent to do so.

There are nuances to all of this, too many to go into detail here, but the takeaway is that the cops cannot simply "look around" in places where there is an expectation of privacy. As a practical matter, searches are limited to the investigation at hand and the information available in the moment.

I'm reminded of a true crime show my wife was watching recently. In this case, a murder victim was found by the police the SECOND time they were at the scene. I told her, and I stood by this, the first time they were there it was based on a report of a *missing* adult. This first visit was a cursory, fact-finding visit, and the possibilities and probabilities at that first point are endless, so the cops are working with the information currently available.

When does a search move from the most likely places to the less likely place? From the house and furniture to under the house and furniture? To the trash piles and the dumpsters down the street? Then the other house, the abandoned houses, the yards, lots, and acres? To the creeks, ponds, lakes, rivers, and oceans?

You and I can holler from the couch to the TV all the things that we would have done, but we weren't there when things played out in real time. Until the police can articulate the decisions needed to go forward in a court of law, with what details they have in the moment, they simply can't.

If our homes are to be safe from government intrusion, you and I are at a near-sacred level of protection from the government. Searching people, more than a frisk, also requires probable cause, and it's allowed once someone has been placed under arrest. A frisk is very limited and is based on the safety of the cops involved. The reasonable suspicion standard must be met, articulated, and defendable before a more intrusive search can take place.

"THEY WERE RIGHT THERE WITH HER AND DIDN'T LOCK HER UP!"

We are funneling into simplicity now: it all comes down to the Bill of Rights, probable cause, and the facts as the murder cops see them in the moment.

There are fewer things more frustrating than letting a prime suspect walk out of your presence because the case just isn't there yet. No wine before its time, though— the constitutional concerns roll over to the trial standard of proof beyond a reasonable doubt. As hard as it is, it's the right thing to do.

So, before you even think about letting your opinion on a person's guilt or innocence fly, imagine letting someone you have evidence gathered on leave your presence. More than your pride is at stake; the safety of the public may be on the line. And you still have to let them walk away. Those are some shoes to try on sometime. But, in the end, you either believe in the intent and letter of the law, or you don't. How would you like the Constitution applied to you?

"EVERYBODY KNOWS HE'S GUILTY, BUT THE COPS WON'T ARREST HIM!"

I doubt you can find a murder cop with any time on the job that hasn't heard this over and over again from survivors and the public.

First, this is true sometimes. Everyone else might know, but until the cops get this info—and the details to prove it—the case stays dead in the water. There are tons of reasons why people don't come forward with valuable case information. They range from concerns about personal safety all the way to "It ain't none of my business." From my experience, it's rarely because of fear; it's usually because of pressure within a culture that says you simply don't rat, even if it's family.

Second, knowing and proving (proof beyond a reasonable doubt and then some) are two very different things.

"THEY DIDN'T READ ME MY RIGHTS!"

MIRANDA WARNING

"You have the right to remain silent. Anything you say can and will be used against you in a court of law. You have a right to an attorney. If you cannot afford an attorney, one will be appointed for you."

Reading of the Miranda rights is one of the most misunderstood concepts in the justice system. Based on the 1966 Supreme Court decision *Miranda v. Arizona*, the police are required to inform individuals in custody of their constitutional rights to remain silent before interrogating them. It's built on the idea that when people choose to speak to the cops, it must be of their own free will and not coerced, nothing more.

The cops can initiate a conversation with anyone, and anyone can decline to participate in the conversation (unless used in stops based on reasonable suspicion, where the cops can ask you to identify yourself). Real confusion comes when people assume that whenever the police have someone in custody, Miranda is required. This simply isn't true.

The *only* time when Miranda is required is when two things are happening at the same time:

- The person being questioned is in police custody or reasonably believes they are in police custody (i.e. that person is not free to leave), and
- an interrogation is about to take place.

If one of these is missing, Miranda will not apply.

If you are arrested and the police do not intend to ask you questions directly related to the charges you face, then they don't have to read you your rights.

If you come to police headquarters and are free to leave anytime you like, the police can ask you direct questions or an interrogation and never have to read you your Miranda rights.

If you are in the car on the way to headquarters, or jail, and start blurting out details about the case against you without being prompted, the cops don't have to stop you and read you your rights—only if they want to start an interview with you. They can use your own unprompted statements against you.

Murder cops get very familiar with Miranda, and when it comes into play because a statement or confession that can't make it past a suppression hearing (a hearing in court where the defense challenges the validity and admissibility of evidence) is useless.

It's just as important to know when Miranda is *not* required so the murder cop can secure a usable statement and never utter the Miranda rights. I have had more than one case where I never mentioned Miranda and hauled someone off to jail for murder after getting a great confession. I later watched the suspect get convicted in trial, using their own words against them. It's not trickery. It's simply knowing the law.

"CAN YOU BELIEVE THIS? SHE KILLED THAT BABY AND HAD THE COJONES TO PLEAD NOT GUILTY AT HER PRELIMINARY HEARING!!!"

Here are the protections of the Bill of Rights again. The first court appearances (like arraignments and preliminary hearings) happen relatively quickly once a defendant is charged with a crime. It's usually a matter of days. Why? Because in the United States we don't want people languishing in a facility (think jail). It comes down to speed. In lightweight cases, guilty pleas may take place. Typically, this is because of agreements worked out between defense attorneys and prosecutors. In fact, if every case filed was headed inbound for trial, the system would collapse under its own weight. Not to mention, there is a certain amount of procedural and restorative justice that can take place outside a courtroom, and that is a good thing.

That said, in heavyweight cases—like murder—the stakes are much higher. A guilty plea at the suspect's first appearance that is accepted by the judge is rare because of this, and pleading not guilty is pretty much run-of-the-mill. In some cases, they don't enter a guilty plea because the court doesn't have jurisdiction (legal authority) to take a plea.

Even as a murder cop, I'm down with this. Pleading guilty at this point would be foolish. Don't be surprised when you see a judge enter a "not guilty" plea for the suspect. This happens especially if the suspect is uncooperative or the court smells problems with mental health, drug addiction, or other influences that could be acting on the suspect. The burden of proof is on the state (the prosecutor) and any defense attorney worth their reputation will push the state to prove the case in court.

A cool thing to note, sometimes you'll see co-defendants and co-conspirators take lighter sentences early in the process. This happens when they have taken deals to testify against another defendant. I always say, "They did the math."

For example, I had two suspects head for trial in a case I worked involving a brutal kidnapping and rape of a woman. One of the suspects "did the math" and pled guilty. He took 40 years. His friend, not a math whiz, went to trial and ended up receiving a total of 180 years of consecutive sentences. When he gets out of prison, it'll be in a plastic bag that smells like a new shower curtain.

Next time you see "not guilty" pleas and strange plea bargains early on in a case, don't get your underwear in a bunch or start swallowing blood pressure pills. Chill out, and watch the show unfold.

WHAT'S THIS MEAN FOR YOU?

First, I hope I've satisfied a little of your curiosity about why things happen the way they do. I want you to understand why speed takes a back seat to accuracy, ethics, and the law—it's all about our constitutional rights.

I know I am scratching the surface of some very deep topics, but you have enough now to get the picture. If you keep things like reasonable suspicion and probable cause in mind, I bet you'll have a different view of cases and investigations. The questions you come up with will get deeper.

Secondly, if you start to work on some investigations of your own, this information can help you color inside the lines. You are not the government, of course, so these don't apply to you the same way they apply to murder cops. But that's not a license to run wild—you still could cross criminal lines. If *you* don't get nailed there, you could easily hurt a case.

It's true, murder cops can't drag people down to headquarters and make them talk, but does anything say *you* can't? (What a scary thought.) The answer is, yes.

While the Bill of Rights protects the people from the government, laws protect people from everyday people. So, while throwing a flour sack over somebody's head in a dark parking lot, shoving them into a van, and driving them to a remote place to hook some jumper cables up to their body to "make them talk" because you are 100% sure of their guilt *seems* like a good idea… the law would argue things like kidnapping and assault still apply.

Does the Constitution restrict you as Citizen Joe from searching people and places? Nope. But bet both cheeks of your butt that there are laws that do.

You not only could jam up a case by having evidence thrown out, but you also could end up charged as a criminal yourself. This can be tricky. If you enter property assuming it's alright (like a big farm), you are still trespassing. Property lines in both urban and rural areas can be very obscure (much like an abandoned house), but it's always somebody's property.

Is the amateur detective or true crimer required to read someone their Miranda rights? Absolutely not; you'd look dumb if you did. But is it a good idea to interview prime suspects and integral witnesses in murder cases? Please think twice.

Approaching a person you *think* is involved in a murder in order to question them is a bad idea. It's not only genuinely dangerous, but you could be smack dab in the middle of a murder cop's approach and blow it for everybody. Not to mention, you're not trained or skilled in the art.

But let's say you do engage a suspect in an interview, and they make some strong incriminating statements. A solid win! Maybe, maybe not.

How do you prove they made those statements?

- Did you (legally) record it?
- Did you threaten them in any shape or form?
- Did you account for their condition at the time, and the environment?
- Did the murder cops know you were taking this on?
- Did you bother to de-conflict with the cops to make sure your actions weren't jamming up another part of the investigation or killing strategic plans the cops have?
- Are you honestly skilled in moving through an interview to know when to lean in or lean out? To talk or be silent?
- Was your attempt successful at all, or did you just put the suspect at a higher level of alertness or vigilance? Did you accidentally remind them they have some loose ends to tie up? Did you drive them underground and beyond the reach of the murder cops?

What would you say to a survivor if any of these things damaged the case? Telling a survivor you are sorry probably won't be enough.

This matters, my crime-fighting friend, because while you're not immediately accountable, you could easily stumble on a landmine or two. There are a lot of bad implications when people aren't aware of these rules. Any shortcutting on the principal protections of the Bill of Rights can throw a potentially great case into the garbage.

One of the biggest ways a true crimer can destroy a case is by getting loud and driving witnesses and suspects underground. Murder cops plan their contacts and meetings with suspects strategically, often taking advantage of a perp's ignorance or pride, or a witness's complacency. If amateur detectives pound on their door or wear them out with questions, the perp or witness goes into a higher state of alert—they might shut up altogether. If a true crime influencer blasts information on the internet that links back to the perp or witness, it has the same effect.

This goes on way too much in the true crime world!

If you steer clear of this, hats off to you. If you *have* done this, it's not too late to think things through and slow down. That is just as commendable.

One more time, with emphasis added: the murder cops don't need potential suspects going underground. Murder cops need a tactical advantage here for truth and justice.

#3 SOME THINGS NEVER CHANGE

Things change, I get that.

That's where American policing is now; the demand for change is out there because times change, and communities change, and policing must change with the wants that come with those changes.

While some things are ridiculous, like, "let's get rid of police," or "defund the police," there is plenty of room to move policing to be better in many ways, and I am all in. I think police departments can do much better when it comes to hiring, training, checking performance, and unloading people that don't belong in the business.

Change in anything should only take place if it's honestly needed and moves things toward good and further away from bad. Changing for the sake of making change or changing recklessly, as a raw, emotional, knee-jerk reaction, is nothing short of dangerous.

You and I can't bend the rules or processes just because we are frustrated—maybe even hurting—because we'll sacrifice a long-term result for a few minutes of what we think is satisfaction. Let's swap out that word *satisfaction* for the word *justice*, and you'll start to see where I am going.

If we look at the time it takes to investigate a case, the demand for accuracy, and the constitutional considerations, we start seeing that it's critical that the fundamentals can't ever be changed. Well, they could, but things would go south quickly.

My point? When survivors, the true crime community, and the public start to get frustrated with what they see as a lack of results in a case, battle cries start ringing out to pressure police departments into more work, shortcutting protections for the defendants, and reengineering the criminal justice system on a whim.

Simply said: it ain't gonna happen. It can't happen. The Constitution and the Bill of Rights must be protected.

Just so we're on the same page, here are a few things that I wouldn't hold my breath on waiting to change. I hope you *feel better*.

SUSPECT AND DEFENDANT RIGHTS

When we get angry, it's easy to wish the worst on people that do the worst things. It would be horrible to short-circuit the rights of suspects and defendants in our justice system because those same rights are also there for you and me. Am I saying you will do something awful one day? No. Your rights are there in case you are ever *accused* of doing something terrible. I think we could do more to support crime victims and survivors in the system, but this can happen without ever taking away rights and protections for the defendants in court.

CONFIDENTIALITY OF OPEN INVESTIGATIONS

Sorry true crimers. This one's got to stay. We all want the inside scoop, the hot skinny, the dirty details. It's a natural and usually harmless curiosity. But in order to protect rights of the defendants, accuracy and fairness must be front and center. Case work has to be protected until it is produced in court, and even then, guidelines will be in place to decide what is seen. This means that statements from police departments will always leave you with more questions than answers. It's not being stuck up or prudish, it's being careful. At most police departments, there are serious conversations about releasing even wanted suspect information for the same reason: responsibility. You'd be amazed how a simple term like "person of interest" is a giant rabbit hole. Specific case facts like methods of operation—details that only perps and witnesses will know—and personal identifying information must be held back. The murder cops, and eventually judges and juries, need to hear those details from only those with first-hand knowledge. A big pain in the butt for an investigation is the false confessor. Sometimes false confessions are blamed on overzealous murder cops in the interrogation room. Sure, that has happened (which stinks) but there are people in the public lining up to come into a police department, tantalize an investigator with a few tidbits, get in the interview room, and land a whopper of a confession. Why would anyone do this? It's hard to generalize for every case, but throw in some mental health challenges, some attention seekers, a good friend or family member trying to take the heat, and voilà, you have your false confession. Now, most of the time an experienced detective will smell something on the statement, which is awesome. But if the would-be villain lays out some very particular details (cuz they heard clues that leaked out) this can get nasty. Has it happened? Yes. A bunch. I recall a huge case involving a serial killer where an employee at a medical examiner's office was caught talking about the details, big details, of an autopsy. Not only did it put the case at risk (a person was arrested and convicted, and his statement was the only evidence), the info made it back to the victim's family before they could hear it from the right folks. Having the intimate details of how a girl was murdered could give a false confessor enough to sound solid. It also arms a defense team with enough ammunition to claim their guy—the one that actually committed the crime—could have made a false confession! Now we have reasonable doubt. Just as lousy, a confused and hurt family was made privy to horrible details by the wrong people, at the wrong time, under the wrong circumstances. Investigative cases are full of very personal information. From personal identifying information (think identity theft), to habits, hobbies, and other, you know, personal stuff. You would be amazed at what murder cops stumble on during major investigations. It was not uncommon to execute a search warrant in a home and come across some kind of sex toy or homemade sex tape. It rarely had anything to do with the case, so it was nobody's business except the victim's, and they definitely wouldn't want it leaked. I'll wait here while you go take care of a few things in your room... Can some of this eventually come out after a case is cleared? Maybe. Until then—and until the people involved get to hear it from the source—let's just keep all of that between us. Information in open cases will always need to remain unavailable. No one is withholding details for the sake of keeping it from anyone, or "because they *can.*" There are genuine reasons why discretion matters. Case integrity must come before curiosity, no matter how well intended it is. Keep in mind that this whole justice business is just that: justice. Anyone eventually accused of a crime deserves a fair trial. Having details of a case out for little more than public opinion will do nothing but taint juries that will sit on the case. This will always be this way, unless the justice system collapses, and justice doesn't matter any longer.

LAWS AND RULES OF CRIMINAL PROCEDURE

Might as well try to move some mountains first because you're more likely to manage that than change procedure. These rules are complex, which is the reason trained and experienced lawyers play in the courtroom sandbox. Once again, people's rights are wrapped up in these rules and procedures. It's not enough to simply know how this works; we must respect it. For example, people charged with murder will always get a preliminary hearing and the probable cause will be tested by a grand jury. No skipping ahead. No cutting in line. Not for me or you.

WHAT'S THIS MEAN FOR YOU?

Do the Constitution, the Bill of Rights, and the rules of criminal procedure affect you as a true crimer directly? Likely not. You're not the government, so these protections usually don't apply. Don't forget, though, that there are laws that might apply and leave you in a big legal jam. Even if your actions are "legal," you could still hurt a case.

The true crime world is intriguing. One of the best aspects is getting to think like a murder cop, theorizing about what might have happened, coming up with a list of what *you* would do if it was your case, and most of all, sharing all of these ideas with like-minded folks.

Be patient. Understand that, in most cases, your questions are not getting answered for very good reasons—so the cases can be successful, and that's what all of us want. Is this hard on a true crimer? Sure. The vague answers and silence drive my wife, Wendy, nuts! But put yourself in the shoes of a survivor who doesn't get all the details, and it puts things into perspective.

I hope you see my sincerity here—there is real responsibility with what we do and say about cases. Always be empathetic, putting yourself in other people's shoes. How would it feel to be accused of a crime you had nothing to do with? You don't even have to be officially charged. Would you like to scroll on Facebook or watch a TikTok video and hear somebody suggesting, inferring, or proclaiming *you* were responsible for a heinous crime? What would it feel like if your personal information was spread across the internet? How fast would the news trucks be in your backyard? And would clients and customers boycott your business? The "cancel culture" is real and out of control; don't be part of it.

Commit to keeping your focus on helping when you can and NEVER causing harm.

#4 THEORIES ARE NOT FACTS

"Make your theories fit your facts, not your facts fit your theories."

This is the first thing a senior murder cop told me when I got to the homicide unit. It was some of the most valuable advice that I ever received. In a world that seems to be giving up critical thinking skills in exchange for confirmation bias, we need to be reminded of the importance of staying objective. Keeping this mantra in mind helps us stay objective and not fall in love with any particular theory we might have.

There is nothing wrong with striking up a hypothesis or two when you are contemplating a case. As a matter of fact, you're pretty much hitting the scientific method. Where this goes wrong is if you ever start to feel, say, overly strong about one of your hypothetical musings. You might turn your hypothesis into a theory and then start loving your theory like its fact. That's when pride closes your mind to anything that might contradict your theory or turn it to crap. Yep, that's pretty much confirmation bias and turning from inquiry mode to advocacy mode. Skepticism is fantastic but rigidity is not a good thing.

When you read about those awful cases where a person was wrongly convicted of a crime and eventually exonerated, the murder cops likely fell on this sword. When someone (on any side) is knee deep in confirmation bias, they succumb to two pitfalls. First, they only look for information that will support their theory. At the same time, they ignore any information that challenges the theory. In heavy-duty cases, they will get angry at anyone or anything that comes between them and their beloved idea.

When I was a brand spanking new cop, I rode with a senior officer named Charlie O'Connell. We unfortunately lost Charlie to a heart attack a few years ago, but one night he gave me some advice I will never forget.

Charlie said, "Davey, you can't argue with someone who is drunk or in love."

I think Charlie was spot on. Whether it's love for a person or an idea, the emotion is blinding. There are days that I watch or read the news and think a big hunk of society has lost its mind. The amount of conjecture, and I mean ridiculous uninformed guessing, about high-profile cases, is astounding—and scary. This includes so-called "experts" (including cops now and then) that offer ridiculous opinions to the world.

It's bad enough if cops get this wrong—the wrong people can go to jail for a long time. When the public starts in, it can damage people's reputations for good and even get people hurt.

WHAT'S THIS MEAN FOR YOU?

So, here's the thing about this. When you reach out to the murder cops to share your theory, they don't want (or have time) to wade through unfounded theories. Leave the murder cops alone. And don't pull a stunt like trying to embellish a theory to make it sound like something more than it is. If it sounds like it has legs (workable and possible) they might have to consider it a lead. Then they will have to follow the lead to lay it down (eliminate it), and that will cost valuable time. That's time that wasn't yours to abuse; it was the time the survivors need to get to the truth. Only bring factually supported information to law enforcement, not theories.

Keep an open mind (even when it feels awkward). Sales are emotional decisions, investigations are not. Fight to stay objective. You'll not only be seen as a critical thinker in case discussions, you'll also be less likely to get in the way of the investigation.

Put a tattoo on your arm that says, "Make your theories fit your facts, not your facts fit your theories." OK, maybe not a tattoo, but I know many murder cops who had signs like this at their desks to remind them to work from an objective perspective.

Last, but not least, if you are working on cases with some goofy clowns that can't get this right, go find a better circus to hang around. They are nothing but trouble.

#5 I HEARD IT THROUGH THE GRAPEVINE

"I heard someone say they heard…" is the simplest way to define this.

Hearsay is any statement made to a witness who, while testifying in court, repeats the statement. The statement is hearsay only if it is offered for the truth of its contents. In general, courts exclude hearsay evidence in trials. The hearsay ban aims to prevent juries from considering secondhand information that hasn't been subject to cross-examination.

Can it be used in criminal court? Occasionally, with a few exceptions, but generally, the answer is no. If statements make it into criminal court, there is a decision at the bench (a judge) that allows it to come in. If an attorney claimed it was hearsay, but the judge let it in, there were likely court cases and prior case law that opened the door. This is based on the right of all defendants to cross-examine witnesses. If we repeat what someone said, but they aren't actually here to answer the other side's questions, it's a no-go.

Can hearsay be used in civil court? Maybe. You'll find it used a little more in lawsuits, but it is still considered carefully.

"What's the difference?" you ask. Aside from the types of penalties in criminal versus civil proceedings (criminal = jail, civil = monetary judgments), the burden of proof is drastically different.

In criminal court, the burden is proof "beyond a reasonable doubt," and in civil case it is the preponderance (weight, amount, or strength) of the evidence. That means that if these burdens were on a scale, beyond a reasonable doubt might look like a number just below 100%. Preponderance is pretty much OK at 51%. Big difference.

"So, you're telling me hearsay has *no* place in a criminal investigation?" Not so fast. It does not belong *in court*—but it can still have value for a murder cop.

Hearsay is usually considered a lead, sometimes a very attractive lead. It simply means putting in a little more elbow grease with follow up. It starts by tracing the statement deeper and deeper, source by source, identifying each person that carried the message—and what they heard—until you get to the original source. If you can. If the result helps the case, all the better. It can be tedious and frustrating, but it's part of the JOB.

"Is the info usually right?" No way, Jose! Get a grip, my wishful thinker! Just like the old game of telephone, the information changes as it is passed along. The fewer the hand-me-downs, the more likely the message stayed at least close to the original. Again, a big source of frustration for a murder cop.

That doesn't mean the intel is worthless. After all, "Where there's smoke, there's fire." We may never find the true origin, but just the process of methodically following it through spins off new leads. Every teensy element of every piece of information must be tested to stand or fall on its own. This, grasshopper, is the art and beauty of an investigation.

What's this mean for you?

What's this mean for our intrepid citizen murder cop working on a case? It means that if you bring the cops statements you've heard, or things people tell you they've heard, be as thorough as you can with the who, what, and when to give it a foundation. Hearsay can lead to huge breaks in an investigation. Though it may not make it to court directly, this information is appreciated.

Unless you supply the information to an anonymous tip line, you'll likely be called as witness to testify, so be ready. In the end, that's what you are, a witness. If you've been careful and documented your activity well, you can play a big part in the search for the truth and justice.

One more thing: your "confidential" sources? You don't have confidential sources. I mean YOU might, but they will have to be named and interviewed and become part of the big case. It's just the way it works. Sorry, not sorry. Remember, defendants have a right to cross-examine anyone who witnesses against them.

#6 AND THE AWARD FOR BEST EVIDENCE GOES TO...

The Best Evidence Rule. An oldie but a goody.

The Best Evidence Rule applies when a party wants to admit the contents of a writing, recording, or photograph at a trial, but the original is not available. In this event, the party must provide a valid reason why. If the court finds the reason supplied acceptable, then the party is allowed to use secondary evidence to prove the contents are legit and use it as admissible evidence.

In a nutshell, and in a perfect community, all evidence introduced in court is as pure as possible. For example, evidence would be original items, not pictures or drawings of items, and be in the best original condition as possible. Items are handled as little as possible, even when they are first discovered. Granted, natural elements like the weather can do a number on evidence, but once it is found, there is usually great effort in preventing further impact on the evidence.

The problem is people are involved in handling evidence. THAT could never go wrong, right?

Untrained people handling, walking on, passing around, or otherwise connecting to items of potential evidence can give even trace evidence theory a run for its money. Something is always carried into or away from every crime scene—unless some yahoo messes it all up. Crime scene tape is there for a reason: no entry, no touchy.

Judges and juries can accept natural things that happen to items of evidence. Hell, this even includes a body with EKG pads, IV tubes, and intubation equipment because those were tries at lifesaving. After that, any and every unnecessary handling starts to walk away from best evidence.

This is why big drug cases, like a large marijuana grow (at least where it's still illegal), usually require ALL the plants and equipment be maintained through the justice process. Same thing with other drugs or duffel bags full of thousands of dollars in cash.

In some jurisdictions, courts may allow for photographs and videos of these things, or large amounts of cash to be deposited in a bank, but these decisions are made after several hearings and are unique to each case. That's how big of a deal this is.

If someone has a screen shot of a text message that looks like evidence, the murder cops will want the original phone. They'll ask for a forensic examination report of that phone and its storage, along with any provider data related to when this text was sent over the magical airwaves. That's just the minimum. Oh, and we'll need that as fast as possible because these things are at more and more risk of disappearing with every passing minute.

WHAT'S THIS MEAN FOR YOU?

First, if you stumble across something that looks important, don't mess with it. Don't dig, move, manipulate, or otherwise screw with it. Do your (safest) best to not let anyone else touch it either. Always ask yourself what the negative consequences could be if you let the cat out of the bag without thinking this through. You may ruin THE evidence. Don't touch it—call the cops.

IF you take a picture, for the love of God please don't run to the internet with it! Get your fifteen minutes of fame doing interpretive dance, or perhaps performing a musical classic on a small wood instrument. Don't splash critical evidence on the World Wide Web. That's not how justice works.

Be ready for the police to examine your phone. They'll ask for consent, but if that doesn't work, they get a warrant and take it. (If they really need it.) When this happens, be prepared for *everything* on your phone to be in an investigative file that any citizen can read once the case is closed.

Funny how all of this loops around, isn't it? Like the weird circle of life. Maybe rethink the pic thing and just call the cops. Original items, in their original condition and location, have the most value in a case.

#7 GETTING EVIDENCE LEGALLY

Ah, the old fruit of the poisonous tree (or worse).

Fruit of the Poisonous Tree is a doctrine that extends the exclusionary rule to make evidence inadmissible in court if it was derived from evidence that was illegally obtained.

Translation: *How* you and I obtain evidence is one of the most important things to keep in mind. If it's not done correctly, it will, at the least, undermine a case and, at the worst, land someone in jail. That someone could be you.

For the murder cop, our guidelines are the Constitution, its amendments, case law, local laws, and ordinances. There are exceptional instances, for example, that revolve around specific situations:

- **Serendipity** (locating something by chance but STILL in a legal position when the discovery is made),

- **Exigency** (in true emergency situations where there was no time for a warrant),
- **Consent** (when the property owner says the cops can search), and
- **Searches** during an arrest, in some cases.

I'm just skimming the surface here—I am sure some experts in the field would have a few other situations to add. No need to deep dive, you get the picture. This is an area of investigations that takes on-going education and experience.

If the cops stay inside the lines, everything should work out just fine. I say *should*, because while there really is no true gray area here, there are opinions and interpretations. And there's the rub for cops. What should be smooth sailing can be a rocky boat ride.

The consequences for cops who gather evidence illegally can be anything from evidence getting tossed out in a suppression hearing, to key evidence not being allowed in court. It can kill the case (or make it more difficult) and cause the cop to lose credibility. It could even lead to Section 1983 claims—allowing people to sue certain government entities and its employees for violations of their civil rights (42 U.S.C. § 1983). These are made in cases where people's civil rights have been violated by the government, a situation the police need no part of, but they must be careful not to ever get there.

WHAT'S THIS MEAN FOR YOU?

For the true crimer hot on the trail of a case, even the most well-meaning, the consequences may be even harsher than those for the cops.

The location of evidence, how you come about it, and how you handle it matters. Remember, the best evidence rule is "no touchy." But since you're going to argue that you might not be able to reach the police, let's talk about what goes down if you actually do grab the evidence.

First things first. While we know the police need a warrant, permission, or a genuine emergency to get on or in private property, if a civilian does not have permission to be there, things could be worse.

Actions by the citizen detective can be crimes—some very serious. Besides being illegal, any actions you take might tip off a suspect. They might suddenly realize there's curiosity. You might run them underground—delaying justice, if not removing the shot altogether.

While the names of crimes vary from state to state, here are some examples and what they might look like:

- **Trespassing or Burglary:** Going into or onto someone's property without their permission starts with offenses like criminal trespassing and moves up if you do something while you're there—like take something you think is evidence or enter or leave with a firearm. Now the offense starts to move into burglary or higher degrees of burglary. It doesn't take much to hit a felony here. Some states, like my home state of Kentucky, have very strict castle doctrine laws (as in, the right to protect your home). It's no stretch of the imagination to see you getting shot, potentially killed. Property rules get tricky in big places like farms, unimproved lots, and abandoned buildings or houses. You might *think* you are good to go, but someone owns it and has an expectation of privacy protected by the law.

- **Theft, Larceny, Tampering with Evidence:** If you take something that is not yours, like when the government seizes things, even if you know it is a key item of evidence, it is also theft or larceny. The more valuable the item, the higher degree of the offense—working its way to the felony level. Maybe the evidence makes it into trial. Maybe. But you will be headed to a trial of your own! Taking, or even moving, an item of evidence could land you in court. In my state, there is an offense for tampering with physical evidence—a felony, that carries a penalty of one to five years in prison! Try having that on your next job application. I dare you.

- **Tug of War (a.k.a. Robbery Including Assault):** We're not talking about playing games, so you don't have to kick a member off your deserted island. This is real. I have to believe this will never happen in the true crime world, but... God forbid, you go to take something you think is evidence and the person you are taking this gem from doesn't want to give it up—a struggle, or tug of war, takes place. Tug of war is actually a use of force to take the object, which is robbery with what we call a lesser included offense of assault. Bad place to be, my friend. These are nearly always a felony.

- **Don't Bug Me:** Recording conversations (phone calls, video, and the like) can be a form of eavesdropping or another crime in most states. It is tricky. States vary greatly on this; there may be rules specifying if someone needs to give permission, should be notified, and how many people can be on the line. In my home state, it's simple: as long as one person is aware (me), I would be good to go. Before bugging your suspect, check your local law carefully.

You may ask, "WHY ARE YOU YELLING AT ME ABOUT CRIMINAL STUFF?!?!?"

Because I don't want any of my true crime friends in a mess like that. Ever.

My best advice? Be careful about being too zealous and moving too fast. If you think you've found evidence, give the police the tip. That way, the cops can handle it legally and things work out better.

One last note I need you to pay attention to: no one, and I mean no one, should ask you to illegally obtain evidence.

It's one thing if you have been hanging out with someone in their home, and you observed something suspicious, and then report it to the police. That is good information. It's a whole different situation if you sneak into someone's house and look around.

It's an even bigger red flag if a cop asks you to do that—or use any sort of sneaky tactics to get evidence on their behalf.

Cops are not allowed to use civilians to get around things like the Constitution and the Bill of Rights. Period. End of story. Acting as a cop's agent will not keep you out of trouble. In fact, it'll get both you and the cop in hot water, besides hurting the case.

If any cop ever asks you to do this, it's flat out wrong, and the police department needs to know that request was made. Now, if the cops put you on the phone and record it during a sting attempt, they will usually know the rules and you will be ok.

Do cops cross this line often? No, but they never should, and I don't want you to be any part of it.

'Nuff said.

Don't break the law to advance a case or a theory. Think things through and make sure you have looked at all the potential conse-quences before you act. And if you are not 100% sure, stop. Situations like these have awful consequences for the case *and* the crimer who thought they could be the hero.

#8 NEVER BREAK THE CHAIN

Once we have found potential evidence and have paid attention to the best evidence rule, handling this evidence gets pretty serious. We call this the chain of custody.

Chain of custody refers to the documentation that shows a record of the control, transfer, and disposition of evidence in a criminal case. Evidence in a criminal case may include DNA samples, photographs, documents, personal property, or bodily fluids that were taken from a defendant or discovered at the scene of an alleged crime. Not only is it important to legally and properly obtain evidence, but also to properly track its every move.

This is one of the reasons you see the yellow crime scene tape go up and people guarding the scene. The cops must account for everyone near this stuff, 24-7. Who touches the evidence, how it's handled or moved, and how it's tested and examined is mission critical. No one should ever duck under the tape unless they absolutely have a legitimate task in the scene.

There were many murders I worked where, even as the lead, I did not go into a scene until the basic forensic processing and documentation was finished. This is a big one that Hollywood gets wrong. But I wouldn't want to watch the murder cop sitting behind his desk, either.

Photos, video, sketches, or drawings are made to accurately record where the evidence was found and its condition. NOTHING should ever be moved, even by the cops, unless there is a genuine reason why it needs to be. One reason could be safety (a gun in the street with a crowd gathering and getting impatient), another could be inclement weather (rain or snow risking reducing the value of the item).

Collecting evidence involves putting it in the right kind of container (there are specific methods of storage for many different reasons), marking the details on the container (including who picked it up), and sealing the container in a way that makes it easy to tell if anyone tampers with it. Like everything else in the world of investigations, there will be a paper trail for thorough and exact documentation of all of the actions we take.

From there? Detailed records will document every single time a piece of evidence is transported, booked into the evidence room, and inspected—by labs, murder cops, defense attorneys, judges, prosecutors… anyone, everyone, every time.

Any gap in this chain can open up a can of judicial whoop ass! Google Mark Fuhrman and the O. J. Simpson case—talk about a lesson in what *not* to do. Fuhrman jumped a wall and grabbed a bloody glove without a warrant (among other things). Another guy took a blood sample from a suspect and then carried it around in his pocket for hours, including while he was back at the crime scene. You could write a textbook from all the things they did wrong. It may have been before your time, but to this day, there are several who believe the mishandling of evidence played a big part in the "not guilty" verdict at the trial.

Is this really an issue? Besides the O.J. case, anyway? The answer is, yes. In many cases, defense attorneys might stipulate (agree) that the evidence in a case was handled correctly and the trial moves on. This usually happens when the police departments and labs have solid reputations for handling evidence. But, if there is ever a question, or the stakes are super high for the defendant, there can be pre-trial hearings where literally every item of evidence is brought to court, and everyone in the chain of custody holds the evidence and testifies under oath to their role in handling it.

This can take forever. I know because I went through it on a capital (death penalty) case. If you can imagine every item and everyone that touched or handled the item testifying, you start to get how big of a deal this is.

WHAT'S THIS MEAN FOR YOU?

Be careful! Know the laws on things like property and ownership. If you stumble upon something of possible value, call the law and back away like its radioactive.

If you are the finder, you WILL be testifying in court as the first chain of custody link, and I want you to shine along with a successful prosecution. Stay out of the chain. Not because you're not trusted, but because it's a difficult enough place for the cops to be, you'll find it even tougher.

If you do come across anything that may be of value, make detailed notes as fast as possible while your memory is good. Speaking of notes… that brings us to our next minefield.

#9 IF YOU DIDN'T WRITE IT DOWN, IT DIDN'T HAPPEN

Documentation wins or loses cases. No case can have too much. It could suffer from useless information, but there is an old saying that if you did not write it down, it never happened. That is how is how your involvement in the case will be viewed in court.

For murder cops, there are two biggies to this. First, after you hook someone up with murder, the trial may be literally years away. These days, two to four years or more is common. Think about how hard it is to remember precise details from your Christmas party that far back. Then, imagine working on many other cases in the meantime. I doubt most people could keep it all straight for that long.

Second, murder cops usually must have a written record to refer to because answers like "I thought," "I think," and "as I recall" can bring on some sturdy cross examination. Courts aren't interested in what we *thought* we did, or what we meant to do. Nor are they interested in anyone who walks in with a memory that is shot. Good note taking and strong writing skills are key.

The case notes should answer any logical questions a reader might have or clearly point to a source where those answers will be found. Speaking of being found, the organization of notes and documents is also super important. In the biz we called this the murder book: big binders with tabbed sections to organize materials. In my unit, every detective used the same structure. That way anyone who needs to work on a case knows where to find the details, including the prosecutor's office. Most of our case files filled multiple 3" binders.

To capture notes with as much accuracy as we could, I, and most of my murder crew, would take notes as we interviewed (often recording as well), then get in our car, drive a block away, and phone our synopsis into a dictation bank. We knew the sooner we dropped a memo for the file, the more accurate our memory would be.

WHAT'S THIS MEAN FOR YOU?

Take good notes and take them right away. Don't procrastinate. Write neatly (or use a digital document) and think about the space you are in. Capture the details instead of assuming the reader will know what you are writing about. You should record the date and time you made your note, the date and time you obtained the information, and dates and times of events you are recording. Keeping things in chronological form helps investigators and lawyers lay out who did what when.

Also, keep your notes in a notebook or file that you have no expectation of privacy in. If you want to contribute evidence or information, you very well may need to turn over your notes (and anything else in your notebook, phone, or computer) as part of the case file—which will one day become public. So, keep those love notes elsewhere.

Imagine having to competently testify three years later from memory alone. Welcome to the court process—just write it all down.

#10 IF IT MAY PLEASE THE COURT...

Ah, court. If we have agreed that the type of justice that matters is the formal one, then a courtroom is where we want to, and should, end up. I am not going to go deep into the specifics of every element of the court system, but there are some general things that are good to know.

For starters, the court system is an arena governed by tons of rules and procedures—for good reason.

We appreciate the requirements for people who work in specialty jobs to be trained and experienced. For example, I might have a basic understanding of a medical condition, but I would never try to do surgery on my own, much less, tell my doc how he or she should hold the scalpel. This is equally important in the courts.

The criminal courts are pretty much a closed system, for the lack of a better term. Only qualified people get to play, and that's a great thing because so much is at stake—including people's freedom. It is extremely complex. If somebody missteps, the whole kit and caboodle can blow up.

We regular Joes and Janes can file complaints and affidavits that can get someone before a judge or jury, but our role stops there. The attorneys, clerks, and judges are the ones that pass people through the system. They do so in such a way to maximize people's rights and keep everything as fair as possible. They are the experts on the processes, the paperwork, the rules on what's allowed, and when those rules apply. As for police, we are traditionally referred to as the gatekeepers of the criminal justice system.

This doesn't mean the public is kept in the dark—remember, we have a transparent system open to the public, with open records (once cases are closed), and a high level of checks and balances.

WHAT'S THIS MEAN FOR YOU?

You can't walk into an active hearing or trial and announce, "If it may please the court…," and deliver your evidence. It just doesn't work that way.

Be educated and realistic about the role you can play in an investigation. For example, you may be able to file an affidavit (a written statement submitted under oath) accusing someone of hurting you or stealing from you and have a judge issue a warrant for that person's arrest or summon them to court. But I don't think you'd ever be able to file an affidavit accusing someone of murder and see it go anywhere.

Petitions are another great way to express our First Amendment rights, to advocate and bring light to things we might think are injustices. Large or small, these requests for a court to hear a case have their specific entry methods too. You'll need to contact the prosecution or the defense and let them evaluate your information and introduce it to the court.

While I am all about petitions for the right reasons, the idea that our system would bend on a public petition is frightening. It's like a mob or vigilante gang—all emotion and little room for logic and balance. There's a reason our court system has gate keepers.

The stewards of the court know the complexity of the system, which explains why a cop might look at you like you have ten heads and keep you at a distance if you show up raring and ready to go. Cops understand how particular the court system is. It's not just a cop thing —prosecutors and defense attorneys work from the same standpoint. To boil it down: you can't get in on your own, and no one is going to take your stuff in on blind faith. You'll have to establish trust, first.

If your information or accusation makes it into court, you will likely be testifying as a witness. Are you sure you're ready? Testifying in criminal court can be intimidating, it'll drive your anxieties through the top of your head.

You'll testify for one of the two camps: the prosecution or the defense. You might have just said "But wait! I'm on the good guy's side!" Well, remember, both the prosecution and defense are "the good guys." They're both there to reveal truths. The side that sees the most potential in your information will snag you up and have you take part for them. For what it's worth, murder cops regularly testify to information in court that looks great for the defense, and we better do just that. The defense gets to see and hear everything we learn in an investigation. We're here to find the truth, and nothing but the truth.

The fancy word for this is exculpatory evidence. Cornell Law School's Legal Information Institute defines it this way: "In criminal law, exculpatory evidence is evidence, such as a statement, tending to excuse, justify, or absolve the alleged fault or guilt of a defendant. In other words, the evidence is favorable to the defendant. In contrast to it, inculpatory evidence tends to stress guilt."

Back to testifying. If one side picks you, the other side may pick you apart. The traditional cross examination is like we see in the movies. Our court system is antagonistic by design, so friendliness only goes so far in a hearing or trial. It may not always be rough, but roughness can't be ruled out. At a minimum, the side that cross examines you will set out to impeach (cast doubt on) your testimony.

Will they lean in and aggravate you? Absolutely they will. It's part of the game, and if you ever needed that representation going to bat for you, you'd want them to play tough as well. When you're on the hot seat though, it feels like a different story. The cross examiner will try to get you off your track and may even make personal attacks, trying to get you to respond emotionally. Just remember, it's not personal, and emotions have no role in the investigation process. Save your feelings for your therapist.

Testifying in court gets easier with practice—murder cops get lots of practice—but the best defense against anxiety and fear is the truth. Stick to the facts as you know them and recorded them, never guess, and never assume. (You know what that does to you and me.)

#11 WHEN FOOLS RUSH IN

Speed has nothing to do with accuracy, and our system demands accuracy. Rushing leads to rushing to judgment, which leads to mistakes. Huge mistakes. Cops know this, but it drives some people crazy.

"Why hasn't an arrest been made?"
"Justice is being denied!"
"Somebody should be in jail by now!"

We talked about these same statements before. One of the challenges all murder cops face is pressure from the public, beating loudly on the chief or sheriff's door. Eventually, that pressure moves to the detective bureau. As hard as it is, the murder cop must ignore that pressure. It pisses some of the bosses off, but they aren't the ones testifying, so tough luck for them.

Society's expectations of investigations are usually based on what people see and hear in the media. An hour-long crime drama only has so much time to cover the storyline (it's not even an hour when you take out the commercials). That's why they get DNA testing in about eight minutes, autopsies in maybe three minutes, and every case lands on a phone call to the detective about eighteen minutes into the investigation. Welcome to TV land. If you don't believe this impacts people, come to court and watch the looks from a jury when they find out all they thought they knew was just not true.

While the do-gooders shouting for answers might think they're helping, they're typically acting on emotion. When emotion comes into the room, the justice system starts to fail. Like just about everything else in life, decisions based on emotions suck. Murder cops intentionally build in time. Not because they are lazy or they don't care, it's just the opposite. It's because they need a mindset that offers the best shot at doing great work.

I mentioned earlier that when I arrived at my first homicide assignment, one of the veteran detectives took me aside on the first day and told me the whole investigative game revolved around time management. Success depends on organizational skills, time management, case triaging and prioritization, and most importantly, intentionally slowing everything down to get the results the right way.

I know for a survivor or true crimer, that sounds awful. Nobody wants to wait for answers. Some might say it supports the belief that cops are lazy, but it was some of the truest and most valuable advice I got when I became a murder cop. As Wild West law enforcement officer and gambler Wyatt Earp famously said, "Fast is fine, but accuracy is final. You must learn to be slow in a hurry."

As a team (damn near like a family), the folks in the murder unit help check one another when they see someone falling in love with a theory and starting to close their mind. What tips us off to a problem? A detective will start to accelerate their pace when it doesn't make sense. No one takes this personally because we trust each other, and we're all committed to do the right thing the right way.

Today, there is a scary movement where people perceive their own uninformed opinions as absolute truth and demand a different court outcome if the verdict doesn't match their expectations. Here comes virtue justice on a flaming rocket. Violent offenders are looked up to as victims, and victims are shamed. Disgusting.

Cops are not going to jail someone just because someone else feels strongly about what happened. Not in this country. Nobody is going to jail because you busted your hump and got hundreds or thousands of like-minded people to sign a petition.

People get charged when the evidence passes the minimum standard of probable cause and prosecutors see a successful conviction coming. All the emotion in the world means nothing if the case falls apart in trial.

If you really want to create distance between you and the cops, wear them out with crying about how slow they are. They will get really quiet. They won't slow down to spite you, but they will back away from you.

WHAT'S THIS MEAN FOR YOU?

This is not a competition; it's not a race. Urgency will come in if there is an ongoing threat of some type, but even then, it will be paced and controlled. Take a deep breath and appreciate the elements of time and intentionality.

If you're a true crimer watching a case from the sidelines, slow down and look for facts instead of theories. Facts are terminal at some point, theories spiral into infinity.

If you are involving yourself in an investigation, slow the f*** down. It's great to get a burst of energy when you get what sounds like a good lead, but control the emotion. You can be fast *or* correct—the two typically don't show up together.

As for murder cops, we tend to temper our excitement. Maybe because we see so many "good" leads turn up nothing. But more than that, we know we have to move at the right pace because it's the right thing to do.

PART THREE
LET'S WORK TOGETHER

CHAPTER 9
LISTEN UP

IT'S one thing to avoid stepping on any of the booby traps. It's another to make progress together. Pull up a chair, whipper snapper. I'm going to give you some old man advice on what *to* do. (That includes you, coppers. Just so we are clear.)

True crimers, I want you on the floor, in the game, giving and receiving respect. And murder cops in the room, I want you to embrace the opportunity. There are three skills that we ALL need to work on to make things better: listening, learning, and building trust. Let's start with listening.

LISTEN

This sounds simple, but unfortunately, it's not. One of the first problems we find between the true crime community and murder cops is communication. As in, it may not even exist. I've spent quite a bit of time talking about the nuances of murder investigations and the nuts and bolts of how they take place. Hopefully, you can see why the time factor alone might make it hard to corner a cop for a conversation. Time and intentions aside, we won't get anywhere if we can't communicate.

There's an old saying that God gave us two ears and one mouth for a reason (I'll pause; you can count). I believe that is true. Bringing two worlds together has got to start by reminding ourselves to listen more than we talk.

Real listening happens when we are not distracted. When we intentionally remove physical, emotional, and other barriers so we can pay attention. We check our biases and engage others with an intention to learn. Most importantly, we are present in the moment, and the people we are listening to know we are listening. When people know we've cleared our schedule for them, they know we regard them as important to us. Intentional listening will support the concept of trust that you will see in a few pages.

If two people approach one another with the goal of listening instead of babbling on with what they want to say, even if they find it difficult, conversations can start. And I'm betting a relationship might begin as well.

The true crimer and the murder cop will both need to find the time to talk. Maybe talk isn't the word I am looking for—we're starting with listening, as in showing up to the conversation in order to listen and learn from each other.

WHO GOES FIRST?

I'm going to insist the murder cops go first on this one, because we are the ones with the vested interest in this relationship we need to build. Not easy, I know. There are times you feel so buried that listening to some outsider is almost impossible, if not a pain in the ass. Here's how I know this to be true.

I could have blown my first murder arrest if I hadn't caught myself being an idiot. I was in the murder bay one afternoon, buried, wrestling with loads of cases (not murders by the way), feeling like I was raking leaves on a windy day. I was pretty cranky, not wanting to be bothered by anybody. (We've all been there.) Someone from our administrative report staff yelled across the counter that someone was downstairs in the lobby demanding to see a detective. Now.

I looked around to see who was going, which was stupid, because since I was the new guy, the looks I got clearly told me that I was the one going downstairs. Great. Wonderful. I started across the floor, hit the down button on the elevator, grumbling to myself as I watched my day melting away with little or nothing to show for it (or so I thought).

I got off the elevator and, as soon as I opened the lobby door, met a rather unkept older man yelling, "I want to turn state's evidence!"

What? Too many movies? So, YOU'RE going to blow my afternoon rambling on about some bullshit that means nothing? I said this to myself, of course.

Here's the deal. He wasn't full of shit. Based on what he told me, I had a murder warrant ready for one of two defendants within minutes of our little talk. I was the one who had been full of shit. I had forgotten that it's the people in the community who solve cases, not us murder cops.

I could have easily shut him down with my dismissive body language. I never came close to screwing up like that again. In fact, it helped me look at people very differently. He wasn't a true crimer, but he could have been, and in my crummy mood, I would have written them off just the same.

My biggest error was not actually listening. He was excited, a little less than literate, and was all over the place, barely keeping his thoughts in place. Not his fault—I was the one obligated to slow down and listen to him intently on *his* terms, not mine.

I get that murder cops are busy, and sometimes busy makes us cranky, but it really is your job to answer the door when the community knocks, and literally welcome them in.

Do everything you need to manage your time: schedule as much as you can, set time limits for meetings, and come with a general idea of the direction you want the meeting to go. But always be kind, undistracted, and respectful.

Be honest murder cops (true crimers, cover your ears for a minute): you and I both know you'd bust your ass to meet with a prostitute or a dope dealer that the narcs just turned if you heard they had a scintilla of information about a case. The true crimer is valuable as well, and probably more reliable.

We know how important it is to listen when we interview victims, witnesses, and suspects, so let's not forget about information sources. When true crimers approach us with information, we need to remember how many times this community has helped in murder cases. Prioritize these people, and purposefully make time in your schedule for them so they know they mean something to you.

Will you always see the ball get hit over the fence for a home run? Of course not. But murder investigations are a game of inches, not yards. Good cases are made with bunts and walks more often than home runs, so get these true crime folks on your team.

One more thing coppers: It's 2024. We all know that the more you engage the community, the better off the policing industry will be.

TRUE CRIMERS, TOO

Listening goes a long way for the true crimer as well. Everything about listening intentionally applies, but we should turn up the volume on that ear for learning.

You have to admit this murder biz you're fascinated with is at the same time a strange place. I took you into that world and showed you just a touch of the complexity. Trust me, there's much more that will remain a mystery—until you learn the ropes.

When you are talking to someone from a police department or sheriff's office, do them the solid of setting time aside, removing distractions and biases, and giving them the benefit of the doubt when it comes to what they say. They are likely teaching you as you go along.

Be respectful of the time you get for a meet-up or a phone call. Have your initial thoughts organized and ready because these first meetings (likely brief) will usually be the "just the facts" conversations.

Remember, the murder cop is trying to evaluate what you have (or don't have), and what your intentions are. Be ready to give an honest answer as to why you are involved. The clearer and to the point you are, the more likely the murder cop will pay attention.

This is never the time to ask questions about the case. Well, you can, but I think you'll be shooting yourself in the foot. Remember, they have no idea who you are. You're not negotiating in a quid pro quo relationship: they are not likely to trade information with you. Get to know them, get them to trust you, and they may one day talk about cases with you, but that's a bit farther down the road.

By the same token, I really can't emphasize enough that you shouldn't be contacting the murder cop asking to simply "run some ideas" by them. They want actionable information.

Maybe you're not a sleuth and simply want to talk to the cops about a blog, vlog, podcast, or other project you're working on. Pretty much the same dynamics apply.

Be specific (and honest) about what you want to do and why. Be ready to share examples of your work. I'm crossing my fingers you haven't been hammering the cops in your place of influence, because that's pretty much the death knell for your request. Speaking for myself, I wouldn't have anything for you either.

If, by chance, they don't stop and talk right then and there, ask if you can schedule time with them. That's still a solid win, so don't get down in the dumps if they won't talk right away.

One last thing about listening: Listening doesn't require us to like the person we are listening to, even though it probably helps. Listening does not require us to agree, either. It does require us to check the emotions that can arise from dislike or disagreement and stay focused on the bigger purpose. In this case, it's justice.

CHAPTER 10
LEARN THE ROPES

I'VE FOUND cops and true crimers have a key trait in common: curiosity. Both camps are always looking around the next corner, eager to figure out what's happening under the surface. If we care about victims, survivors, and bringing about true justice (and I believe you do), then we need to care about our craft.

One of the most rewarding experiences as a murder cop was that I was *always* learning something. Many days it felt like it was coming at me like a firehose, but I loved it. I tackled my college undergrad and graduate degrees as an adult because I love learning new things.

Learning doesn't have to mean formal education. Are you curious? Do you listen to experts? Are you reading this book? Good. Glad you got one.

Learning the ropes is about more than how to do our own jobs, but I want you to grow there, too. It's also about learning how we can work together. Understanding, appreciation, and respect grow when we also take time to learn more about the other side.

COPPERS, LET'S START WITH YOU

My law enforcement friends, you know I get the challenges of formal training and how scarce it can be. Don't let it stop you. Get all of the training you possibly can, and don't forget to train on things beyond the tasks you are performing today. It's never too early to start learning for the next level or assignment. I know you're hit with budget and staffing issues, but push for more training every chance you get.

You don't have to wait for formal training. Learn on your own. One area I'd like to see murder cops dive into—and this one is free—is the world of true crime. Podcasts, blogs, vlogs, you name it, tap into some! You'll find some faithful storytellers who research cases in great detail and deliver the information to audiences beautifully, often with an educational perspective. You'll find genuine victim advocates, as well.

Now, I'll warn you, you'll find some pretty stinky stuff too: people who have an overly morbid fascination with murder, those who exploit the plight of the victim and survivors, and, of course, the anti-cop armchair quarterbacks. There's good and bad out there for sure. If a true crimer contacts you and asks for an interview, be sure to check out the individual and their work so you can avoid giving time and energy to the fools.

You see enough of the bad guys—sometimes it's good to remind yourself there are good guys in the community too. Find out what everyday people are doing right. Search online for instances where people in the community have helped provide answers or moved the ball forward on investigations.

For example, check out an amazing group of scuba divers called Adventures with Purpose. They locate submerged vehicles in bodies of water and frequently find the bodies of missing persons, some cases that have been unsolved for many years, and they go about it the right way. This group is a prime example of the gifts that time and virtuous motivation can be, and it's not in a police department.

TRUE CRIMERS, IT'S YOUR TURN

You probably aren't planning to turn your life and career into being a sworn murder cop. That's OK. But there's no reason you can't pick up some knowledge and skills to dive deeper. Learn to question, learn the process of justice, and speak from a position of knowledge. When you do, you can add to the conversation about a crime instead of distracting or causing a trainwreck. A few things come to mind for me that I would look at doing to sharpen your brain saw a bit.

SHARPEN YOUR CRITICAL THINKING SKILLS

How often do we stop to analyze, think things through, and ask important questions? These days, we're more likely to be scrolling sound bites (a.k.a. TikTok and Reels) and zoning out. Where have all the thinkers gone? No really. This is key.

When I was working on my degree, one of the requirements for adult learners (old guy back in school) was a class called Critical Thinking 101. My classmates and I were a little miffed that we had to pay for and spend time on such a silly class. On the first night of class, we asked the professor why we had to be there. Her answer made me a little sad—apparently, today's college students show up lacking critical thinking skills. Ouch. Just in case you missed them too, let's start at the beginning.

My favorite definition is from *The Foundation of Critical Thinking*:

Critical thinking is self-guided, self-disciplined thinking which attempts to reason at the highest level of quality in a fair-minded way. People who think critically consistently attempt to live rationally, reasonably, empathically. They are keenly aware of the inherently flawed nature of human thinking when left unchecked.

The keywords that stand out to me include reason, quality, fair-minded, rationally, and the big one—unchecked.

Another way to understand critical thinking is to approach things with an open mind—maybe more than open—perhaps a bit skeptical and loaded with questions that challenge every scrap of information we come across.

The word *self* in that definition is important, too. Critical thinkers are "self-guided" and "self-disciplined." If you were a cartoon, you'd have thought bubbles all your own.

Sure, we could wind up hanging out with people who are like-minded and think critically, but the only way to know if that's happening is to pick up our own critical thinking first. Why? Because whenever two or more people get together, the risk of groupthink skyrockets. Unless the group is deeply safe and trusting, no one will challenge other people's theories, ideas, or opinions. The person with the power, or the loudest voice, sets the "truth" while everyone else nods, cheers, and blindly follows.

Critical thinking prompts us to ask reasonable and respectful questions about the information we receive before we regard it as factual or meaningful. For example, when you hear someone detailing a case, especially one not even on trial yet, are you suspicious?

Pause and ask yourself these questions:

- Who are the people making the claims of innocence or guilt?
- Who would have something to gain by seeing information released to the public prematurely (as in pre-trial)? Is the other side commenting? Why, or why not?
- Where is the evidence? If it's even available, how much is there?
- What are the champions of this cause basing their story on —facts, or emotions? Are people letting their emotions get hijacked or confusing feelings for facts? Look out.

The truths in a case will be found and confirmed in the courtroom. Every other speculation and opinion is potentially folly. And for the record, remember everyone is viewed as "innocent until proven guilty" in court.

Watch press conferences and media coverage with an open mind. I don't care which channel you watch, don't automatically take it as fact. Ask yourself a few critical questions:

- What hurdles are the investigating agency facing? Is this a high-profile case, like is a child involved? Are there multi-jurisdictional considerations? (Remember that contract with bigger agencies thing.) Is there public or government pressure?
- Do they need to protect sensitive information? Again, are there kids involved (victim or suspect)? Are they preserving evidence? Do they need to keep the bad guy from running underground?
- Who might benefit from the particular version of events that is being described? Are there points being made that seem unrelated, but are being stressed regardless?
- Is a timeline being presented in a logical order, and does it add up or make sense?
- What is the media outlet's reputation for objectivity? Unfortunately, many major news sources are more opinionated than we would like. Ratings and clicks sell.

Keep that open mind of yours. Be the curious kid constantly asking, "Why? Why? Why?"

EMOTIONAL INTELLIGENCE: WHERE DO YOU STAND?

If critical thinking is the driver, we can't forget to have emotional intelligence riding shotgun. How well do you know yourself? Not how you *feel* about yourself, but do you know who you are? How does this affect you when you're around other people?

Let's look at this definition from Verywell Mind:

Emotional intelligence (EI or EQ for "emotional quotient") is the ability to perceive, interpret, demonstrate, control, evaluate, and use emotions to communicate with and relate to others effectively and constructively. This ability to express and control emotions is essential, but so is the ability to understand, interpret, and respond to the emotions of others.

Knowing who we are, what we feel, and how we perceive the world means a great deal when it comes to being able to communicate and work with others. EQ is the magic that we use to work with people we don't always agree with. And for a true crimer, understanding your strengths—and blind spots—will help you if you ever hit up a murder cop with information. First impressions matter. If you come at the cops with a loud and proud distrust or damning attitude, you're gonna be off to a rough start.

Part of emotional intelligence includes our ability to self-reflect, the skill that helps us learn about our triggers, biases, pet peeves, strengths, weaknesses, and the like. Let's not forget that we should always be reaching inside to status check our motivations, our integrity, and our ethics. They play a big role in how others view and, ultimately, judge us.

Murder cops use their EQ every day working with people from all walks of life. It's the bread and butter of how they can build fast and meaningful rapport with people they don't know.

Your EQ will determine how others see you, if they will trust you, and if they want to get to know you. Like everything else in life, none of us will ever be perfect at this, but working to improve sure goes a long way. There are tons of great books out there to get a grip on this and grow your EQ.

HOW DEEP DO YOU WANNA GO?

What you choose to learn and how deep you want to go is up to you. It's likely based on your role and goals.

If you identified yourself back in Chapter 4 as the *Interested* or the *Curious*, I bet you'll find learning the real world of investigations to be a blast. You'll find yourself taking details in and analyzing cases differently. Most true crimers have a healthy curiosity about how investigations work, and they love discovering the details.

For the true crimer with an unhealthy interest in this business, well, therapy would be a great first step.

If your motivations are virtuous and you fall into *The Influencer*,

The Advocate Activist, or *The Amateur Murder Cop* categories, then by all means, get started NOW. The more you know—legitimately know—the better you will do and the less likely you are to get in trouble or delay justice in a case.

I can offer some suggestions on topics and sources—and I will—but first, let me offer some advice.

Wherever you go to learn, it has to be the real deal. True crime shows and documentaries are interesting, entertaining, and make for fantastic conversations, but very few are truly objective or sourced with any authenticity. On the podcast and YouTube channel I produce, *The Murder Police Podcast*, it is authentic. Of course, we want to capture the listeners' and viewers' interest, but the content is always grounded in authenticity and an educational mindset. Unfortunately, very few in the podcast and entertainment world use that approach.

Not sure of a show? This is where critical thinking skills are handy. Start asking those heavy-duty questions: What's the motivation of the show? Does it invoke emotion or answer questions objectively? Are all sides and all the data being presented? In a nutshell, if your objective mind is asking more questions than you are getting answers for, there is a problem. Find a better source.

I hate to say this because some people may get offended, but here I go. There are people in the true crime biz who have been around it a long time. They may even be successful at hosting and producing shows, or writing blogs or books, and may even land gigs adding color commentary (their opinions and interpretations of a case) on documentaries and TV shows, but they are *not* subject matter experts (SMEs).

Be picky. I can't tell you how many times I've stumbled across this time-equals-expert mindset on the internet. It blows me away. I think it's more than a coincidence that these folks are usually close-minded, super defensive, and cannot be reasoned with. Take this for what it's worth, but even if I tell them, "Hey! I lived this and know what I am talking about!" they will try to trump me. Wow.

So, how can you learn more? Here are eight excellent ways to dive in deeper:

1. **Take an Actual Class in Criminal Investigation and the Criminal Justice System.** Colleges and universities will offer degree programs in fields related to investigations. As part of getting those degrees, the schools will have course catalogs full of amazing topics that get students closer to degree completion. I have taught criminal justice and related college classes for several years and I have never seen one that I would complain about. In most cases, schools hire teachers who have experience in the field, which is a solid win. If you are not looking to get a degree, check out certificate programs. Too much? Some schools might simply let you pay for a single class and take it, while others may allow you to audit (sit and watch) the class for free. I have had the privilege to be an adjunct professor teaching these classes over the years and will vouch for their value and credibility.

2. **Intern.** Some colleges and universities offer credit for intern programs with law enforcement agencies in the areas they serve. Holy cow! You read that right. You are actually imbedded in the agency for a front row seat and usually get to help out on some of the tasks being performed. The agency I worked at did this and moved interns through a variety of detective units, including forensic services.

3. **Hit the Books.** If the school option doesn't work right now, grab some used textbooks and read them. Finding used textbooks in university bookstores or online is a snap, and the prices are usually affordable. As an adjunct professor, I never saw a textbook that I didn't like. Some have fantastic exercises and review questions to stir your brain a bit. Bonus: no tests. Look for books that introduce you to the criminal justice system, criminal procedures, investigations, and forensics. Pick up a couple and you'll wonder why you waited so long. I would look for the most recently published

edition you can find, especially if they speak to advancements of science or technology. Head over to *The Murder Police Podcast* website at www.murderpolicepodcast.com and look for Murder U (short for Murder University) to find my recommendations for learning more about the murder cop biz.

4. **Pull Some Real Cases and Read Them.** If you are in the biz of podcasting, vlogging, blogging, or writing about true crime, this may not be new to you. Then again, I may be about to help you up your game quite a bit. When you are really interested in how these murder cases are put together, you can ask for a copy of the case (files, notes, pics, videos, and recordings) from the agency that completed the case. The keyword in most cases is completed, as in cleared (closed) and prosecuted.

Case files offer quite a bit for the reader:

- You can learn more about how investigations are conducted, recorded, and memorialized.
- If you are storytelling, you'll come from a point of verifiable accuracy. This is handy for your reputation in the true crime community and for liability protection.
- If you are looking into a case post-investigation, this will be your cornerstone as you move forward.

Obtaining case files is done through a Freedom of Information Act (FOIA) request or an Open Records Request to the investigating agency. These vary somewhat from state to state, but they are all based on transparency (as in the right to know how our tax dollars are spent).

Cases that are open will *not* be available because there is still work to be done on the case. Open cases are just that: Open. Under investigation. Protected for the justice system. It doesn't always mean they are active (like we want them to be), but they remain unavailable. Even cold cases. There are very rare times when an incredibly old case (as in, no one is likely still alive) might get popped open, but again, it is *rare*. The information needs to be protected in order to safeguard the integrity of the investigation and pursue a fair trial.

You may ask, "Then, what is a closed case?" Even if you didn't ask, I going to tell you anyway.

The Uniform Crime Reporting (UCR) system, and its child (when everyone finally adopts it), the National Incident Based Reporting System (NIBRS), looks at investigations in one of three ways. As cases are reported by the agency responsible and with the jurisdiction regarding the latest status of that case, they will be designated in one of three ways:

- open
- cleared
- cleared by exception

Hint, hint (since you are into clues), did you notice that "pended" and "cold case" are not on that list? Hmm… that's because those are still *open*.

Once a case is closed, some information (primarily personal identifying information) will be redacted (removed) before it is made available. Also, in many states, images of a graphic nature will be withheld.

I'm down for that. I've seen too many sickos distribute gruesome crime scene photos of victims. That's simply bullshit and unneeded. If you do have access to graphic material like that, don't be a douche, don't put it out there for everyone to see.

Hey, and for that matter, be responsible with what you get, period. Just because people's names might be in those files doesn't mean they need to be put on blast.

5. **Ride-Along.** Many police and sheriff's departments offer opportunities to ride a shift with a patrol officer. I really

recommend this if you don't have much experience with law enforcement. As a patrol officer, I carried several ride-alongs. Every person left the car at the end of the shift with a completely different view of what cops do than they had seen on TV. In a ride-along, you'll experience cops who are people and see them for who they really are. You'll likely be exposed to some very real situations, possibly tragic, so be prepared for that and how you will deal with it. And who knows, you might get the bug to pursue a career in the police biz.

6. **Citizen Police Academies.** Known as CPA for short, these programs have been around for decades and are phenomenal for getting truly immersed in the experience. Typically, an agency will host a handful of academies a year. The educational program runs for multiple weeks, meeting one evening a week. A coordinator lays out an incredible schedule of behind-the-scenes experiences: participants tour police facilities, hear officers speak on their unique specialties (think murder cops), and get practical experience. Officers lead them through things like making traffic stops, conducting building searches, crime scene processing, and sometimes even simulated shooting systems. Your speed and judgment are tested under (safe) pressure. Talk about an eye-opener! Oh, by the way, the murder cops in most CPAs will deep dive into some of their real murder cases, taking you deeper than the general public. Why? You've built trust and rapport with the family as a CPA attendee.

7. **Volunteer.** More and more agencies are adopting civilian volunteer programs. Volunteers may be asked to help with a variety of things, from reception at the front door to making follow-up contacts with crime victims. Just think about how much you could learn doing this.

8. **Get a J.O.B.** Finally, I have to make this pitch—get a job or start a career at a law enforcement agency or related industry. Personally, I recommend becoming a sworn member (an officer) and working toward being a detective because I loved my career so much. That said, if it's not the fit for you, there are several fascinating roles in law enforcement agencies. Each one of them will challenge you and give you the satisfaction of doing truly meaningful work in your career.

Some examples include:

- Attorney (defense or prosecution)
- Forensic Lab Technician
- Forensic Specialist or Scientist
- Paralegal Professional
- Police Officer or Detective
- Psychologist
- Social Worker
- Victim Advocate

I am sure I missed some, but no matter the precise role, you'd be in the eye of the storm, on top of the hot skinny every day, and part of an amazing family. Give this some thought.

Making a difference, from inside or outside the system, will only come when we listen to each other, challenge ourselves to keep learning, and build trust. That last one may be the hardest yet. Turn the page, and let's find out.

CHAPTER 11
TRUST

I COULD BE MIXING up the chicken and the egg here: Is trust built between people who will listen to one another? Or do people who trust one another listen better? Either way, no one's going to work together effectively without trust.

We toss the word *trust* around a lot. Sometimes it's assumed, and sometimes it's broken. It's one of those things that is super hard to earn but so easy to lose. I think trust alone—or lack thereof—is the biggest hurdle between the true crime community and the real detectives. It lurks just beneath the surface whenever the two worlds try to communicate.

ONE LEVEL AT A TIME

We don't need a deep, vulnerability-based trust in order to get started. A simple working trust will do. This starts by knowing and understanding the systems and methods more than it does knowing the individual people involved. With a little work, great relationships and trust can certainly come along, too.

If you are simply an *Interested* or *Curious* crimer, a little working trust can help you bypass your biases. Get to know and respect the systems and methods, and you'll come off as more in-the-know and educated in your opinions and analysis of a case.

But if you want to be involved in investigations, at some point you're going to want to take your findings to the police. Like I have said, the murder cops need everything in as good of shape as possible. They have to work within the criminal justice system. That listening and communication thing we just talked about? That's the path that makes all this work.

I know, trusting the United States criminal justice system will be a tall order for some folks. Add the media's portrayal of it, and yes, the occasional snafus we see, and it's extremely hard to trust it. But then again, finding or building trust is always difficult. The more you try, the easier it seems to lose.

Since when are you a scaredy cat? Stop running away from risk. Let's sit down for a second and look at a few angles of attack for this problem:

Trust in the System: Can both sides mutually trust the system at its core? I'm not talking about how it always plays out, but at its foundation and intention. This isn't about trusting individuals in the system (yet), but can we stop using the exceptions (when conduct is straight up wrong) as the rule and stereotyping everyone in the system?

Relational Trust: Once we get the system on board, can we narrow the focus and start to trust the actual people that are part of it? And can those members trust the people outside the system? This is where the real progress will come; it's going to take a ton of work and time to build these relationships. Be persistent and be patient.

Vulnerability-Based Trust: The pinnacle of trust. Author and consultant Patrick Lencioni describes this as trust found when people are smart enough and have the courage to be real with one another. They can admit they do not know everything and admit when they are wrong. They're willing to learn from one another instead of holding the other at a distance. If we can move from trust of the system to a working trust with those within the system, we should all continue to work toward the deeper trust.

————

THIS IS IMPORTANT

If you, as a true crimer, trip up on purpose or by accident, you'll likely be deemed unreliable. Untrustworthy. Any good work you might have done could go unnoticed. And you'll likely be frustrated, if not downright mad. Murder cops, I am going to ask a lot of you folks again as well. There are good people in the true crime community. I strongly suggest you work on trusting people who simply want to help.

————

If we could remove the individual involved when things didn't go right, I'd venture to say we'd actually agree the US system is still the best justice system in the world. Take a look at our Bill of Rights (I put it in the back of the book for you).

I hate to tell you this, but if you are questioning the entire system on go-wrongs that are outliers, and you're letting your emotions get hijacked, then *you* are stereotyping.

There's no place for stereotyping in an investigation. It's a blind spot you need to work on. You might even be suffering from groupthink. You know, the bandwagon you jumped on. Don't ever forget that the band occasionally plays out of tune.

If you stacked up all the wrongs committed by judges, jurors, prosecutors, defense attorneys, cops, witnesses, and pretty much anyone else who breathes near a courtroom, you'd still be left with a narrow piece of the pie in the chart of good and bad in the justice system.

WHY IS TRUST SO HARD?

Good question. If we look at what trust is based on, we begin to see the hurdles that we have to deal with.

I scoured the internet (academic slang for Googling) to get an idea of the basics of trust. As I expected, there were lists of anywhere from three to eight foundations, acronyms, and letters in 3s. Some overlapped. Some dove deeper than others.

I found five core tenets of trust that spoke to me. Both sides, the true crime community and the murder cops, ought to do their part to build these.

Reliability

Are you someone people can count on? Do you do what you will say you will do, when you say you will do it?

This hallmark of trust begins when we provide accurate information to one another, no matter which side you start on. If you think there are questionable aspects in the details you've been told, be candid. Ask your questions from the beginning.

Reliability continues with basic actions: return calls and emails as promised, and follow through, as best as possible, when you say you are going to do something.

If you're truly motivated for the right reasons, guard against the destructive forces of ego. Own your shortcomings and make amends for the mistakes you make.

We all extend more trust to people whom we can rely on.

Honesty

This should be a no-brainer. Never lie. Never put lipstick on a pig. Never try to turn a dog turd into a cherry pie.

Murder investigations are often loaded with brutal honesty, and they must be. For a murder cop, any uncertainty or misperception of the truth can cause emotional hijacking. The same goes for those in the true crime community. In most cases, murder cops don't dust the truth or the status of an investigation with fairytales and wishful thinking, because that fuels those notions already in play with survivors and increases pain. Understanding that is a must. Be careful about supporting narratives that are based on wishful thinking, conspiracy theory, and confusion.

Remember what I said about CIs (confidential informants) and honesty? If a CI, who's usually paid for their work, ever lies—even one time—they not only won't work as a CI for that detective again, but they are flagged in the department's system for life. They'll never be used again.

True crimer, hear this: if you ever lie, withhold info, or otherwise deceive a murder cop, you're toast. You might even be in hot water legally.

If the murder cops lie, they are supporting the negative narratives and stereotypes some people believe about the police. No one wins.

We all have to remember that no one wants a case to suffer as a consequence of dishonesty.

Goodwill

This is all about motivation and intent. Go back and read the list in Chapter 4. Cops are constantly evaluating information sources. This doesn't just apply to in-person interactions, either.

Pay attention to how you posture yourself on social media. Do you come off as an attention seeker? Are you so done with law enforcement that everything you say and post is through that lens?

Murder cops will see through smokescreens; they'll pinpoint crummy intentions and distance themselves from anyone who comes at them with questionable motives. And for good reason. When it comes down to backing up things like affidavits for search and arrest warrants, or testifying at hearings and in trial, they will not—and should not—have to answer to those issues on your behalf. At best, you'll give off an icky vibe, at worst, you'll hurt a case.

Competency

This one can be a hot potato. Before we start debating the grading

system, let's start by clarifying which type of competence we're talking about. Here's the definition Merriam-Webster dictionary gives.
competence: *noun*

a. possession of sufficient knowledge or skill
b. legal authority, ability, or admissibility

Definition (a) is pretty straightforward. Do you have the knowledge, training, and understanding to do the job? You wouldn't want a first-year med student performing your open-heart surgery. They don't yet have the competence.

Definition (b) covers mental competence; as in, is the suspect sane or insane? Someone better get a psych eval before he takes the stand. It also covers things like old grandpa signing that new will, even though he has dementia. Did he understand what he was doing? Will his signature hold up?

When it comes to building trust in working a case, you better have (a) or you could really screw up (b) for everyone.

- Find some evidence and break the best evidence rule or chain of custody? You're done.
- Go on someone's property without permission, armed only with your righteousness, and commit trespassing or a burglary? You're done.
- Record a conversation or make a video without the other person's knowledge in the wrong state? You're done.
- Set up a trap to catch someone? Entrapment may not apply because the government didn't get involved, but $5 says your work runs the risk of getting silenced in a suppression hearing, and once again, you're done.

Fair or not, the standards in the justice system apply to everything that is presented in the system. Your "good intentions" mean nothing if evidence is considered tampered.

The murder cops know this. They live this. And they sure aren't going to risk anything that looks like they don't know what they're doing so you can be the hero.

Cops train for this. They made it through the academy, the criminal justice degree, the trainings and tests to get to where they are. They've worked too hard. They're fighting stereotypes, doubt, and criticism every day. And they are focused on doing a deep and thorough investigation that will hold up in court. Otherwise, the bad guy is just going to get away with it.

True crimers, if you want to be trusted, you've got to learn some of the ropes to the legal system and listen when you're asked to stay out of the way. Go back to that list of learning opportunities and ask questions. You gotta do things legally, or you're only going to cause more harm. And a cop has to trust you.

Openness

The mack daddy of trust relationships: being open, vulnerably open. No other trust can compete with a trust built on being completely open. Humility, social intelligence, accountability, and grace. There is much to it, but your best relationships, like with your help-me-bury-a-body friends (gotta talk true crime talk), are based on these qualities.

I am not going to pretend that true crimers and murder cops will necessarily achieve this one, but working on it will make a relationship better and trust come easier.

It starts when we admit we don't know it all, understand our own biases, and put them in check, ask for help, and own up to mistakes without blaming others.

PRO TIP: When the murder cops work with survivors, this is where they build a relationship. It's more than rapport, it's about showing the survivor they care about them and that they're in this for the long haul. Is this possible for the true crimer? I think so. Speaking personally, I have stayed in touch with informants from decades ago because we developed relationships. Some have walked a life that many people look down on, but once they trusted us and we trusted them, we witnessed acts of bravery and character that few people would ever see.

I've also seen these deeper trust relationships develop with private investigators (PI). This trust didn't come with their PI license issued by the government, or because of some classes they took, or what they were able to charge. They worked hard and earned it through their motivation, humility, reliability, and professionalism.

Trust should never be assumed. Never forget that it's hard to earn and super easy to lose.

WHERE DO WE GO FROM HERE?

Have a little faith in the system. Learn it and work with it, not against it. There's nothing like getting involved to actually improve account-ability. Talking heads make a lot of noise. It's the people in the trenches who make things better.

If you're a true crimer who wants to make that difference, this trust with the murder cops is where the rubber meets the road. It's not the same as trusting the justice system. This is a relationship—more of a quid pro quo—and it's full of biases on both sides.

It's going to take an open mind. There's a reason a lot of people don't trust the cops. We've been programmed not to trust the police. This doesn't come from any one political side. Policing gets screwed, blued, and tattooed from every political front—if there's a potential to gain votes by dumping on cops, politicians dump away. And it's not new, by the way. It's been this way since policing started in this country, and it shows no sign of slowing down.

The distrust works its way through virtually every media and enter-tainment outlet, mostly because it sells. I challenge you to find five major motion pictures that portray law enforcement in a good light and did well at the box office. Good luck! Most paint pictures of systemic corruption or stupidity. In a culture lacking critical thinking skills, the narrative people are spoon-fed becomes their vision of reality.

Coppers, we have to admit some of this has been brought on

ourselves. There are times we feed the machine. As Uncle Ben told Peter Parker, "With great power comes great responsibility." We won't be perfect—we're human. But we sure as hell better try. We cannot forget the tenets of trust: reliability, honesty, goodwill, and competency. They matter. Fight for them. Because every simple mistake or misjudgment of a situation erodes them. Not to mention the occasional criminal behavior. Yes, I just said that because it needs to be said. I can work with mistakes because we all make mistakes, but I can't work with crooks and assholes.

Keep in mind that failures (real failures, not people's biased perspectives) in the criminal justice system are rare. The system does have safeguards in place that usually catch the error. It may take time, but the errors usually come to light. Let's not throw the baby out with the bath water.

True crimers, you've got to know that cops rarely trust anyone. This isn't because culture feeds them a line, their experience with the worst of the worst from all walks of life proves it—over and over again. I don't care if you're a bona fide saint, you're going to have to prove you're trustworthy. So don't take it personally.

Do put in the effort to build trust. Do check your motivations and be honest about your intentions. If the murder cops can rely on you, you'll probably even find a little grace when you do make a mistake. They may even stay connected and give you a little advice to help you keep moving forward.

To my cops still here, we (and no, I don't have a mouse in my pocket) need to keep more trust doors open for the true crime world. I know what it's like to be disappointed. I can still feel the sting of being lied to and watching promising leads dissolve in my hands. If we can accept that we don't magically solve cases because we are wizards or witches, then we can be open-minded about the folks in the true crime community who want to help. They are a resource that needs to be recognized for its potential value.

Why? Because victims matter. Survivors matter. That's who we're all here for, after all. Let's risk a little more and build trust for their sake.

CHAPTER 12
TIME IS ON YOUR SIDE

HAVE you ever watched NASCAR racing? Everyone thinks it's all about speed. Sure, the first car across the finish line wins—but if you pay attention, you'll find it's really all about strategy and teamwork. The smart teams know when to slingshot and when to pull in for a pitstop.

Murder investigations aren't any different. Yes, we want to catch the bad guy. But you've got to play it purposefully. Reckless speed isn't going to get you anywhere other than in a pileup. Even in cases where the police think they have someone dangerous at large in their community, the detectives stay systematic and methodical, making sure they color inside the legal lines. Evidence won't bring justice if it's inadmissible in court.

As a true crimer, you don't need to be in a rush either.

Whenever you're uncertain, feeling like there must be more to the story, or hear your intuition yelling from the back of the room: stop! Put on the brakes and pull over for a minute. Don't let our instant, on-demand culture or pride get in your way.

It's as simple as *waiting* to comment on or share a sensational post until you've done a little research and formed an educated opinion.

It might mean *pausing* before you roll up your sleeves to investigate a case yourself. Make sure your questions aren't going to tip off a suspect or add pain to a survivor.

Remember, the consequences are real. So be careful.

The old "beg for forgiveness instead of asking for permission" thing won't fly for you. As much as my teenager likes to use this tactic when it comes to curfew, laws are laws. "I'm sorry," won't get you out of jail.

Calling the murder cops for advice isn't likely to get you anywhere either, because they don't want to assume any liability or responsibility on your behalf. If they could talk, I bet you the first thing they'd say would be to slow down or stop. Would you take that advice?

Like I said when I started, this is a big, complex, and very real world. When it comes to criminal investigations and the search for justice, the goal is about helping victims and families. They are real people and there are real consequences for screwing up.

Take your time. Listen and learn. Be helpful. Build a little trust.

Whatever you do, don't hurt the cases or the survivors.

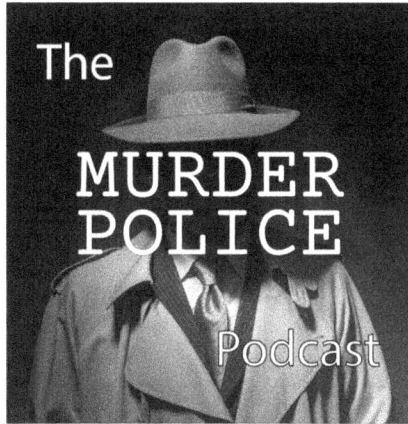

TRUE CRIME. REAL DETECTIVES.

You know the headlines…now hear the stories behind them. *The Murder Police Podcast* pulls back the tape and lets real detectives walk you through the cases that kept them up at night.

Follow now on your favorite podcast player or on YouTube—and scan the code to get inside access and exclusive updates from Wendy and David.

Because some stories don't end at the crime scene.

BILL OF RIGHTS

The Bill of Rights is made up of the first 10 Amendments to The Constitution of the United States. It lays the foundation for civil rights and liberties for the individual, such as freedom of speech and the press, protection from unreasonable search and seizure, and the due process of law. They were ratified by three-quarters of the states on December 15, 1791. Every citizen should know their rights.

THE BILL OF RIGHTS

First Amendment
Congress shall make no law respecting an establishment of religion, or prohibiting the free exercise thereof; or abridging the freedom of speech, or of the press; or the right of the people peaceably to assemble, and to petition the government for a redress of grievances.

Second Amendment
A well-regulated militia, being necessary to the security of a free state, the right of the people to keep and bear arms, shall not be infringed.

Third Amendment

No soldier shall, in time of peace be quartered in any house, without the consent of the owner, nor in time of war, but in a manner to be prescribed by law.

Fourth Amendment
The right of the people to be secure in their persons, houses, papers, and effects, against unreasonable searches and seizures, shall not be violated, and no warrants shall issue, but upon probable cause, supported by oath or affirmation, and particularly describing the place to be searched, and the persons or things to be seized.

Fifth Amendment
No person shall be held to answer for a capital, or otherwise infamous crime, unless on a presentment or indictment of a grand jury, except in cases arising in the land or naval forces, or in the militia, when in actual service in time of war or public danger; nor shall any person be subject for the same offense to be twice put in jeopardy of life or limb; nor shall be compelled in any criminal case to be a witness against himself, nor be deprived of life, liberty, or property, without due process of law; nor shall private property be taken for public use, without just compensation.

Sixth Amendment
In all criminal prosecutions, the accused shall enjoy the right to a speedy and public trial, by an impartial jury of the state and district wherein the crime shall have been committed, which district shall have been previously ascertained by law, and to be informed of the nature and cause of the accusation; to be confronted with the witnesses against him; to have compulsory process for obtaining witnesses in his favor, and to have the assistance of counsel for his defense.

Seventh Amendment
In suits at common law, where the value in controversy shall exceed twenty dollars, the right of trial by jury shall be preserved, and no fact

tried by a jury, shall be otherwise reexamined in any court of the United States, than according to the rules of the common law.

Eighth Amendment

Excessive bail shall not be required, nor excessive fines imposed, nor cruel and unusual punishments inflicted.

Ninth Amendment

The enumeration in the Constitution, of certain rights, shall not be construed to deny or disparage others retained by the people.

Tenth Amendment

The powers not delegated to the United States by the Constitution, nor prohibited by it to the states, are reserved to the states respectively, or to the people.

ACKNOWLEDGMENTS

There are so many people to thank for leading me to writing this book. In most cases, they never knew they had inspired and encouraged me to take this on.

First, the victims of violent crime that I had the privilege to serve: They had no choice, really. No one ever chooses to become a victim. Those who died as a result of a crime certainly didn't get to choose me to solve the mystery. However, in the wake of their death, I was blessed to become their voice and to wade through a very untruthful world for justice. Those who did survive acts of violence didn't get to pick their cop, but I will always be humbled by the trust they had in me as we walked an incredibly frustrating path together.

The survivors: I owe a debt of humble gratitude to the people left behind after a death at the hands of an evil person. Families, friends, and loved ones get life-changing news that cuts like a razor, leaving wounds that bleed forever. My heart can only imagine the life they must live "after" and refuses to put my feet all the way in their shoes. I could add up all the pain I might have faced in my life, yet it will never compare to theirs. Anyone who thinks the life of a homicide detective —a murder cop—is glamorous would learn quickly that it is the most humbling of roles in public service. And it hurts. Forever. Thank you to all the survivors I got to know and love, even if our paths crossed in the worst way to do so.

My mentors, leaders, and partners: This is a large group of people in the cop community; in most cases, they are all three in one. Long before I wanted to join the murder police, I watched people in my agency do amazing work and carry themselves in remarkable ways. If I tried to name everyone, I am sure I would accidentally leave some fine folks out. Some hardly knew my name, yet I knew them by their reputation and seeing their names on reports in case files. I tried hard to be who they were.

My leaders in the murder cop community: To those who showed me what trust, patience, and wisdom looked like, from all levels of supervision and command in the investigation bureau of the Lexington Police Department in Lexington, Kentucky. Thank you to Dan Gibbons, Fran Root, Anthony Beatty, James Curless, Brenda Cox, Marvin Devers, P.T. Richardson, and John Dixon. My Lord, call me super blessed. I hope everyone gets "bosses" like these. There were so many more outside investigators who were amazing as well. Thank you.

My partners on the team: No single murder cop makes a case. Decades later, I remember all those long days and nights, the disagreements, the ridiculous jokes, and the crap we handed each other. I'll never forget the laughter in the old crime scene truck, maybe caused by carbon monoxide (because of a slow exhaust leak), but nonetheless, lots of laughter and dark humor helped us unsee the worst of the worst for a moment. And the incredible humility we shared as we learned from each other every day. It's how we survived the hard days, the occasional bad leadership, and the constant hum of pain in the investigation of the taking of a precious life.

The silent partners in investigations: These people—who walk a life most look down on—were, in reality, some of the strongest people I have ever met. Thank you for coming forward, sometimes at great social or physical risk, to help the murder cops and simply do the right thing. Informants, CIs, snitches… call them what you like, but the other murder cops and I respect them incredibly and stay in touch with some years down the road.

The final spark: I have to thank a student, Daisy Waites, in the United Kingdom. She reached out to interview me for a project she was working on in 2022. We messaged and met for a Zoom interview when Gabby Petito came up. Daisy asked thoughtful questions about the public's involvement (or injection) into the investigations, and it got my mind turning. The curiosity and open mind that led her to speak to someone in law enforcement ignited the fire that set this book in motion.

My editor: *If* this book is readable and you, as my reader, get the impression I can stitch words together and spell correctly, then I have to give that credit to my wonderful editor, Tara Cooper. Recommended to me by the author of Silence Kills, Scott Harvey, Tara approached my manuscript from a wide perspective that I could not have managed, and offered countless valuable suggestions as well as critical corrections.

If Tara Cooper helped make an impression that I can write, then Empowered Press Publisher Jill Carlyle will make people think I know how to publish a book. I don't, as in no clue whatsoever. However, Jill does, and I am grateful to have met her and signed on with Empowered Press. If you, my reader, ever head down this road, find Jill, give her the keys, and let her drive.

My support system: My wife Wendy, an insatiable true crime fanatic, is my partner in crime on *The Murder Police Podcast* and in my life off the air. Wendy tugs me, sometimes less than gently, back into my career with endless questions and whys. She was our podcast avatar, and neither one of us knew it for years. Wendy is my love, and I am a better person for having her in my life. When I married Wendy, I gained a fantastic stepson named Jasper Tate Faircloth. I met Jasper when he was a tiny six-year-old (the same age I knew I wanted to become a cop), and his imagination and fevered interest in the cop world kept my love for the job alive. Thank you both for sharing and supporting this life and passion.

My inspiration: And finally, the one person in my life that likely never knew she was making huge sacrifices, my daughter Brooke Elizabeth Lyons (Allen): Cops' families make sacrifices every day in the forms of worry, concern, time away, missed holidays, and vacations that often never happened. For a murder cop, the foundation of their love and support literally brings us home. Our families are beyond precious. Brooke, just by being my little girl, reminded me to be empathetic and to work hard for people who had lost loved ones. Brooke was there at home with hugs, kisses, dances, and her smile. She will never fully appreciate the strength she gave me when investigations got rough, cross examinations on the stand wore me out, and when I had to work under difficult leadership in the police department. I'll never forget the day I got on the stand to testify in a difficult murder case that was built on a lot of circumstantial evidence, and when I turned the pages in my murder book, there were her doodles—bringing me back to what really mattered most. What a gift. Love you, doodlebug, all the moon and stars.

NOTES

PREFACE

Dunning-Kruger Effect and the four stages of competence: Therapist.com. "Dunning-Kruger Effect." Updated May 15, 2024. https://therapist.com/behaviors/dunning-kruger-effect/

CHAPTER 3

Moving pictures and the first use of special effects: "History of Film," Wikipedia. https://en.wikipedia.org/wiki/History_of_film
The invention of talkies: "Radio, Film, and Television," Wyoming History Day, https://www.wyominghistoryday.org/theme-topics/radio-film-and-television

CHAPTER 5

The number of full-time officers in police departments: "Census of State and Local Law Enforcement Agencies 2008," Bureau of Justice Statistics, report published July 2011, https://bjs.ojp.gov/data-collec tion/census-state-and-local-law-enforcement-agencies-csllea#2-0

CHAPTER 8

Reasonable suspicion and Terry Stop: Searchandseizure.org, "Reasonable Suspicion," http://www.searchandseizure.org/reasonablesuspicion.html

Probable cause: Searchandseizure.org, "Probable Cause," http://www.searchandseizure.org/probablecause.html

Proof beyond a reasonable doubt: Merriam-Webster.com Legal Dictionary, s.v. "reasonable doubt," https://www.merriam-webster.com/legal/reasonable%20doubt.

Miranda: Legal Information Institute of Cornell Law School, "Miranda warning," https://www.law.cornell.edu/wex/miranda_warning

Hearsay: Kelly, Alexis. "Hearsay in Criminal Cases." NOLO. https://www.nolo.com/legal-encyclopedia/hearsay-criminal-cases.html

Best evidence rule: Legal Information Institute of Cornell Law School, "best evidence," https://www.law.cornell.edu/wex/best_evidence_rule

Fruit of the poisonous tree doctrine and illegally obtained evidence: Legal Information Institute of Cornell Law School, "fruit of the poisonous tree," https://www.law.cornell.edu/wex/fruit_of_the_poisonous_tree

Evidence chain of custody: Just Criminal Law, "Chain of Custody and Why It Is Important in a Criminal Case," August 26, 2020, https://www.justcriminallaw.com/criminal-charges-questions/2020/08/26/chain-custody-important-criminal-case/

Evidence for the prosecution or the defense: Legal Information Institute of Cornell Law School, "exculpatory evidence," https://www.law.cornell.edu/wex/exculpatory_evidence

CHAPTER 10

Adventures with Purpose: https://adventureswithpurpose.com
Critical thinking definition: The Foundation for Critical Thinking,

"Defining Critical Thinking," https://www.criticalthinking.org/pages/defining-critical-thinking/766

Emotional intelligence: Cherry, Kendra. "Emotional Intelligence: How We Perceive, Evaluate, Express, and Control Emotions." Updated January 31, 2024. Verywell Mind. https://www.verywellmind.com/what-is-emotional-intelligence-2795423

CHAPTER 11

Competency: Merriam-Webster.com Dictionary, s.v. "competency," accessed May 17, 2024, https://www.merriam-webster.com/dictionary/competency.

Appendix

The *Bill of Rights*, Amendments 1–10 to the United States Constitution: United States Creator. *Bill of Rights*. [Place of Publication Not Identified: Publisher Not Identified, -09-25, 1789] Image. https://www.loc.gov/item/2021667570/.

ABOUT THE AUTHOR

David Lyons is a former homicide detective and retired police commander, living in central Kentucky. In retirement, he focuses on two passions: One, his role as a faculty member with FBI-LEEDA (the Law Enforcement Executive Development Association), the other, producing *The Murder Police Podcast* and *The Murder Police Podcast* YouTube channel.

Cohosted by his wife Wendy Lyons, the show's mission is to memorialize victim's names on the internet and tell their stories through the lenses of authenticity and victim advocacy.

Find us on your favorite podcast player, on YouTube, and at murderpolicepodcast.com.

www.ingramcontent.com/pod-product-compliance
Lightning Source LLC
Chambersburg PA
CBHW052019030426
42335CB00026B/3209